BRANDON WARD SR.

The Pain of a Man

A Story of Perseverance and Becoming Stronger Through the Pain

First edition

ISBN: 978-1-7350486-0-4

Cover art by Germancreative

This book was professionally typeset on Reedsy.
Find out more at reedsy.com

Contents

PROLOGUE

I pray that this book reaches you right on time. Special thanks to Melancholy, a sculpture created by Albert Gyorgy, which portrays the void that grief leaves us with. The sculpture is in Switzerland. During the beginning of my writing journey, I reached out to Albert after coming across the sculpture while surfing the internet. Everything about this historic piece of art spoke to the way I was feeling. Empty inside, strong on the outside. Surprisingly, Albert returned my email with very encouraging words. I made sure to relay to him the inspiration for his art, which has inspired me to tell my story. This project began as a therapeutic experience, fighting all the demons from my past. I needed a clear picture and remember of all the things God has gotten me through on this journey. As men, we rarely show our feelings and express our true thoughts. Very few are unaware of the mental battles we, as men, fight in this world. Not to mention the unforeseen challenges men face, that to this day remain invisible. We all have been born in different circumstances and situations, not realizing that the experiences we have during our childhood create barriers that must be overcome as we mature. Whether you are born in struggle or privilege, everyone has their battles. Many of us fall on our journey and it feels as if the world just keeps moving forward without us. Many have lost everything and never bounced back. The fall of a Man can happen in many forms and different ways. We can fight till death, but once a man loses his dignity and pride, it is like losing his soul. The feeling of helplessness and loss of control is a constant inner battle. Every day, every minute, and every second, you are constantly thinking, "How did I get here? Why do I feel like this? Who can I trust? Why me? How do I get back to normal? Followed by those thoughts that the mind subconsciously knows all the true answers. Turning into self-sabotage. These thoughts alone are a heavy burden that builds stress, causing us to find ways to suppress and cope, only numbing ourselves in the moment. We find many ways to do so, picking up what we need to get by, and never putting it back. Only adding to the difficulty of "Getting back to normal."

We, as a community, do not realize how poor our mental health can get and to get better it takes time. Time to heal, recover, plan, and take appropriate action. I lost a very close friend due to the avoidance of his mental health. A person that I confided in with everything. This man is incredibly smart with discipline that one can almost envy. One of the most hardworking men I knew. Being a former Marine and Purple Heart recipient. Being a man who obtained his master's degree, to the man that now will not say a word to anyone, including me. There was a time that we spoke three or four times a week for hours. However, after a disagreement between women, his fiancé demanded that he no longer had any lines of communication with me or my family. This concerned me because as a Veteran I knew what my buddy was dealing with internally regarding his PTSD. There were many nights that I talked him off the ledge and the bottle. Now that he no longer had me, who will be there for him to fill that void? No one. A year later he has been in and out of the psych ward, became a mute, socially distanced himself from everyone he loved, only to now be found walking the streets of Las Vegas. Even in temperatures exceeding 110°. He does have a decent apartment, with interior that speaks his pain for him. Uninhabited and frigid. When I visit, he lets me in, and does not say a word. Which is not normal for a man who at one point in his life would continuously give the soundest advice. I do not complain because after two years of being a cop in Las Vegas, I have seen the worst outcomes of many things. Many men honestly do not make it through their storm. Many give up or become a suspect to their own murder.

At this very moment of writing this, it is amazing to observe my thought process of trying to figure where exactly to begin. The mind wants to express so many of my current feelings and emotions, which at this point and time serves as a distraction. I guess I will ask myself a question as if I was in an interview, and the first question is "What was the defining moment of your life?" I must pause and meditate on these thoughts, as many thoughts arise within my subconscious mind. As I investigate my past; many moments have defined me collectively. Many of those moments have included joy, success, and pride. As well as embarrassment, anger, pain, exhaustion, and tragedy. Which led me to discover my sex addiction. Which I used to suppress my pain and boost my ego. This book is all-inclusive and a guide to my decision making whether right or wrong, and the action taken or procrastinated that led me to success or missed opportunity— but if I had to pick one, it would be the worse night of my life, and how "The Universe" used me to be heroic and save the life of my daughter Brazyl, and witnessing my six year old daughter's life almost taken by a hit and run driver, leaving her in grave condition. Turning our world's upside down.

I am writing this book for those men going into their storm. For the man going through their storm or coming out of a storm. As a man who has been through a few storms myself and persevered, I can guarantee you that you can too, and you will. Let us grow!

1

TRICK OR TREAT

Waking up Halloween morning 2013, joy was in the air. The night before, I had just got back in town from a business trip from San Antonio that I cut a day short just so I could be with my family for the holiday. The children were excited to see me and could not wait for me to get home so they could put on their Halloween costumes and show daddy. Brazyl was a pink power ranger, which defined her personality perfectly. Strong, athletic, smart, and fearless. BJ, age eight, was the red power ranger. Equipped from head to toe, they came downstairs showing off their latest karate fighting moves. Kicking and punching the air while saying "HIIEE-YAA". Pretty much mimicking every move they watched on the show. They were the most adorable crime fighters the world has ever seen in my eyes. They were excited and I was a proud papa. My wife Tiffany of seven years at the time, was happy to take our children to pick out their costumes while I was out of town. The costumes were a great idea because they would be extra visible for the Halloween night. She even bought our daughter Berlyn, 22 months old, a costume as super girl, which was adorable as ever. They were super excited about the holiday and I was happy to be home so I could share the moment and create family memories with them.

As the children awakened in the morning, they came downstairs to their costumes on the head of the couch. Their school was having a Halloween parade that allowed the student to show off their costumes for the night. I love events like this because as a parent, I need my children to get as much normal use of the costume as possible including the night of Halloween. Plus, it gives us parents an opportunity to take pictures and show them off to our family, friends, and the world of social media. Tiffany, who was the photographer, had a mini photo shoot in our living room. The children had taken plenty of photos, kicking, and holding their leg up, trying to balance on one leg, fight pose, and taking a defensive stance— but there was one photo that stood out. It was strong, it was fierce, and it showed Brazyl posing with a fist and BJ in fighting stance in the background behind her. The photo would soon be all over Las Vegas and we had no idea.

That morning the children went off to school, Tiffany and I made sure we would be home for work in time to make necessary preparations and get the kids out for a Trick or Treating early as the sunset. The plan was to walk to the neighborhood church that Berlyn attended for daycare. They had been advertising their Trunk or Treat yearly event that they put on for the safety community. We agreed on our route and decided that we would visit the houses in the neighborhood on the way to the church, attend the event, and visit a few houses on the way home. Now, this was the perfect plan to get us home in time to catch the 4th quarter of Thursday night football game between the Bengals and the Dolphins, and I had my bet in on the Dolphins and the over. The game started at approximately 6 pm western Pacific time. We got ready and left home late during the first quarter. The score was 0-0 at the time so things were not looking good for the over. Bored with the game I was excited to see the joy on the children's faces— they were anxious for the night.

All packed up with Berlyn in the stroller, we headed out staying on our side of the street and visiting our next-door neighbor. Every year their teenage children turn their garage into a dark creepy haunted house, get dressed in super creepy costumes, and spent the night busy scaring mommy's, daddy's, princesses, and superheroes. As we went through the children were frightened clinching my leg for safety. It was apparent Brazyl looked to me to provide safety. I stood by her side as I pushed Berlyn in the stroller through the haunted house, past the vampires, witches, clowns, strobe lights and smoke. As my girls were screaming, I let out an evil laugh to intensify the experience. Then it was over. Just like that. A lot of fun for small space. From one side of the garage to the other. As we exited, we thanked our neighbors for the fun and continued up the block. There were many times where Tiff and I would just watch BJ and Brazyl interact and lead each other. We would let them approach the door and yell "trick or treat", and then, we would follow with the baby's bag, which was for the two of us. Don't judge me! I remember a neighbor specifically giving Brazyl extra handful of candy for the sole purpose of how nice, patient, and kind spoken she was. After hearing such a great compliment, Brazyl ran to us and told us with gratitude and joy in her eyes. By the time we made it to the church, it was busy. They had carnival games, a jumper, food, music, and good vibes. Although, we were not members of the church, we had acquaintances from the daycare. We had a great time and they had plenty of candy to hand out. We may have stayed longer, but Brazyl brought it to my attention that she still had homework that she needed to finish so it could be turned in the next day. I look back at her and all I could think about was how proud of her I was and her will to succeed. Just two weeks earlier, she was awarded the Frank Kim Elementary October Student of the Month Award. As a first-grader, she was getting it. Very smart and determined to succeed. Brazyl inherited that approach from my grandmother raising me. My motivation was to make this wonderful woman proud and keep her proud. My Grandmother showed me that my success and best effort was enough to bring her joy, and I was the same way with Brazyl, determined to manifest that feeling. She after receiving her graded assignments or projects, would always return them with a bright red scarlet letter A. We would have her take pictures and post them on social media, then place the assignment on the success shrine located on the kitchen refrigerator with magnets. She had the fridge full of assignments.

As we got ready to leave, we said our goodbyes to a few people and met with another family from the neighborhood. Brazyl and their son both attended Frank Kim and knew each other, but were not friends. We had enough similarities to develop rapport and were headed in the same direction so we decided to see the caravan as we proceeded home. As we exited the parking lot and headed towards the street Brazyl was ecstatic, saying "This is the best Halloween ever." As we headed towards the street, there was a car coming from the distance driving at a high rate of speed. This was a silver car driving much faster than the posted 25 mph speed limit. This car appeared as if it was racing another, and as it passed us we were all upset. From a distance we saw another car approaching, but I can only see two bright headlights that were damn near blinding. This car had to be traveling much faster than the other, and we were all committed halfway into the street. The engine was roaring and the headlights were approaching at light speed into our crowd. Everyone dispersed and you hear a loud bang. I immediately check myself and baby Berlyn as I was pushing the stroller. I see Tiffany, I see BJ, and I see Brazyl approximately 100 feet laying on the ground not far from the stopped (Black) vehicle from my recollection, with a Hispanic looking young man behind the steering wheel. At this point, everything seems to be mute, but I can hear every sound necessary and relevant to the situation. It was like I was in and outside of myself. My first reaction, my first thought was to run and snatch the driver out of the car and beat him to death for the actions of his negligence, which has now caused my family the deepest level of pain. For turning our entire lives upside down. I already knew, in that moment, there is a lot of pain ahead of me. I cannot believe this SOB hit my daughter! What the Fuck! While charging at this car, as my anger builds to its highest peak with every stride, I turn to my right and my heart sank. I see my baby girl's lifeless body in the street. I direct my stride towards her. Within the same moment, just like that, the driver was gone. The man sped away, and I am left to fight for my daughter's life.

I could hear Tiffany on the ground crying hysterically, completely losing it. The baby was secured and safe in the stroller which was in the custody of someone nearby. Brandon was safe with attendees of the church and laying on the concrete was Brazyl, not moving at all. I completely put all my attention on her and checked for a pulse on her carotid artery. There was none. I then checked for a breath or any air circulation and there was none. At this point, all of my training had taken over. I adjusted her body feeling for any blunt force trauma or bleeding. Finding none, I proceeded to open her airway by tilting her head with her chin up. I positioned myself beside her and administered two breaths while watching her chest expand with air. After delivering her 30 compressions while counting to myself, I am also hearing someone advise me that they had called the paramedics. I gave her two more breaths watching her chest expand and proceeding to 30 more chest compressions and two more breaths. Not good enough, she would need more. At this point, I was exhausted and helpless. I remember saying a quick prayer to God and seeing Tiffany on the floor screaming, "Not my baby!". The driver and the car were still at the corner— I continued with 30 more compressions and two breaths. Brazyl's eyes opened as she took a deep breath, gasping for air. I kept her airway opened and checked her pulse. It felt as if her vein was vibrating with a burst of energy. Her heart was beating what felt like a million times a minute. Pumping hard to catch up, but she was clearly unconscious. Breathing while her eyes remained open. There was a doctor at the scene who stood by and encouraged me through the process. At that point, I was praying internally listening for the faint sirens of the paramedics to increase in volume. God please keep her stable until they arrived. The scene was chaotic. I was surrounded by hundreds of attendees from the church trunk or treat event onlookers crying emotionally. I remember people rubbing my shoulders for comfort. One woman walked over to me saying "I got the son of a bitch's license plate!" Another attendee is saying they have a description of the vehicle. I was just focused on Brazyl's chest expanding and expecting the sounds of the sirens getting closer.

It felt as if the paramedics took forever to arrive. What I say took 10 minutes to arrive, reports I've read say the paramedics arrived within three and a half minutes. Whatever it was, they arrived just in time. As the sirens got close to us, what was once a faint noise was now uncomfortable to the ears. I remained by Brazyl's side until the paramedic exited the truck with equipment in hand, and pretty much tagged me to take over. The paramedics immediately began rendering aid. The fire department arrived shortly after, I stood nearby observing all their life-saving efforts. Tiffany and I somehow found our way towards one another. I began to pray knowing that at that time I was helpless. The paramedics loaded Brazyl onto the ambulance and asked what parent would be riding with. We looked at each other, hugging and consoling each other as we searched for strength. As I looked into Tiffany's eyes and felt so much pain, but she was willing to ride in the ambulance. As the ambulance leave the scene with sirens blazing, all I could do was sit on the curb with my mind in a daze. I literally just sat there as people approached and consoled me. I couldn't say a word, I couldn't move, all I could do was think and pray— and all I wanted was for Brazyl to make it to the hospital. The scene was ugly and very active. There were many police officers searching the area for the driver. The helicopter was hovering around, there was yellow caution tape, many witnesses. Brazyl's Power Ranger glove and pink shoe lying in the middle of the street, which was also covered in scattered Trick or Treat candy. I noticed the news casters as they arrived and figured there was no way I was doing an interview. I gathered Brandon and Berlyn, stood up and one of my nearby neighbors safely brought me BJ and Berlyn to his home to settle down. The children's faces showed horrific pain. Looking worried and traumatized. For the remainder of the time that we were at the scene they stayed glued to my hip. At that point, all I could do is pray. I prayed that God would get Brazyl to the hospital alive. I just needed her to get there and have a chance of living. I knew if she could get there, she had a chance of surviving. I had yet to hear from Tiffany and she had yet to answer her phone. I was lost, but I immediately had to snap out of it and put a plan together to get the children child care and I have to take a ride to the hospital. There was no way I was in the mind state to drive, but I had to get to Brazyl. My first call was to one of my closest friends who I knew no matter what he was doing, would drop what it was, and come and help, and that was exactly what Nick Dunford did. Nick was a former employee of mine that I had hired in 2010. He was a former Marine and Mason with qualities that no other man I've ever met had and is brilliant. At a time, such as this, I knew that could depend on him.

After talking on the phone to Nick, we decided he and Jonalyn would come to the house. She would stay with the children and he would take me to the hospital. Tiffany had not yet called to inform me if they had made it, but Nick and Jonalyn were on their way. As we got out of his truck the man said something about God that was inspirational. Sounded like something out of the Bible. I acknowledged him and he said he would pray for us. I acknowledged him with a thank you and got the baby and the stroller. BJ walked beside me as we walked to the front door. Candy was falling to the ground I didn't give a fuck. I fumble the keys trying to unlock the door. As I struggle with the keys, 8-year-old BJ took the keys from me and opened the door. It was cold, I adjusted the temperature on the thermostat and walked upstairs with Berlyn. As I walked down the hall, I remember it being so silent. In this moment was feeling of pure tragedy. The aftermath of tragedy. It's a somber, draining, useless feeling. A feeling that all you can do is tap into the energy of faith and surrender to the situation. If not, a human being will be opened to all kinds of negative energy that will attach to itself and start slowly destroying your life, due to decisions that do not align with their beliefs or purpose. I walked into the room and the memories of Brazyl were everywhere. Her toys, her shoes neatly placed in the corner. Her favorite pink bedspread and pillows to match. I immediately felt myself losing it inside, but with Berlyn in my arms, I couldn't show weakness. I had to show strength, but I also had to show I had faith. As I got BJ and Berlyn ready for bed, Nick and Jonalyn arrived and rang the doorbell. We went downstairs, told them we didn't have any update, briefed Jonalyn about the kids, and left to go to the hospital. I called Tiffany and she told me they arrived at University Medical Center, and Brazyl was still with us. She told me to hurry. She loved me and then began crying. I could feel every emotion she was feeling just through her voice. I had only heard her sound like that one other time, and that was after she got into a head-on collision. That driver just like this one, ran away from the scene.

We spoke briefly and she needed us to end the call. While in the car with Nick, it was dead silence. I badly needed someone to talk to and get encouragement, but Nick wouldn't say a word. It was like he refused to give me the "Everything is going to be ok speech." I didn't know if he had no hope or just did not know what to say at this moment. All I know is the silence was the last thing I needed. It was a familiar feeling that I had when experiencing something in life and received silence from those I looked up to for resources or mentorship to guide me to make the right decision. But with so much on the line, I just rode in silence and just thought to myself of how life used to be, and how in the hell could I fail my daughter? How could I allow something like this to happen with me present and right by her side? How could I not protect her and endanger her life? Why her and not me? What did I do to deserve this? Would she make it and if she makes it, what would her mind be like after not breathing for so long? We arrived at the hospital and the paramedics that's transported Brazyl was parked in the emergency lane. I got out of the vehicle and ran into the door. I immediately saw Tiffany and embraced her. My mother also arrived with her boyfriend. While holding Tiffany, the door Brazyl had entered in had opened. You could see what appeared to be eight medical staff members attending to her. A couple of minutes later a tall white man with glasses walked out and introduced himself as Dr. STERIT. He said Brazyl was very sick and in bad shape, and in order for them to save her life and preserve as much physical and mental ability as possible, they would need to perform a craniotomy. Removing a portion of Brazyl's skull to prevent the brain from swelling excessively and contacting the spine, causing her to become paralyzed or deceased. For the doctor to be giving this report, it meant she had a chance, and that was all we needed to hear. Just enough to have more optimism and more faith. We shook our heads and thanked the doctor— went into the waiting room and waited. I don't remember us really saying a word to each other. We just waited to get the results of the surgery. We waited and waited for what seemed like an eternity. Not sure how long we waited, but when the doctor came from the back, all he could say is, "Your daughter is a very sick girl." I remember thinking is that it? Is that all you can say? No shit, I know she is sick. The doctor then told us Brazyl had a 10% chance of survival and she would be placed in a medically induced coma until further notice. 10 PERCENT! For others that may have meant the worse, but for me, it was music to my ears singing a song of hope. My reaction to the news was relief. Although part of me was thinking negatively, another part of me had just a little more hope, but I must admit I was beyond terrified. I was terrified by every update that medical personnel provided.

After surgery, Brazyl was admitted into the Pediatric ICU. They have her in the room directly across from the nurse's station. Usually, the patient who receives care in this room requires extra attention, and the charge nurse could monitor all behavior and attend to the person immediately if need be. When they first brought Brazyl into the room they were extremely busy. Tiffany and I stepped out of the room till things calmed, and met with the LVMPD Detective over the case. He interviewed us both separately. During my interview, we had a very difficult exchange. For some reason, at the time I remembered very little and could not answer concrete details. I remember telling the detective what little I remembered, but I was adamant that the car was black in color and the driver appeared to be Hispanic or white with a beard. At this time, the detective stopped me and advised me that the witness had said the car was gray or silver. When I said I was sure it was black, he advised that witness statements described a black car, but that was the car that drove by the scene twice after the accident. I was now doubting myself. Could the car have been silver? Maybe, but not by my account. The detective was compassionate and assured that they were doing everything necessary to find the driver and the vehicle. We discussed hypnosis which I declined because my impression of it was that it was fake. They needed something solid and they were reaching out to the public for help, hoping someone had seen or knew something and would provide a tip. The news began requesting an interview and an update. Tiffany and I saw this as the perfect opportunity to spread the word throughout Las Vegas and influence someone to come forward with more information, or for the driver to become so emotionally unstable because of guilt that he would eventually turn himself in to the authorities. The problem was neither Tiffany nor I were capable of doing the interview that night. The weight of emotions was too heavy so we declined asking them to come back in the morning. Every news station in the Vegas Valley had called the hospital requesting an interview. Although we declined, the news covered the story, and that night every station was telling the story about the six-year-old little girl who was struck by a hit and run driver. The crazy thing is that there were two other accidents that night. My phone had over a dozen missed calls, which I had no intention of answering. I called my manager to advise him of the accident and I would need to take an extended leave of absence. He was devastated by the news, but was even more disturbed because he received a call that one of my employees was involved in an accident causing death to the other party and he thought the two accidents were connected. They too were at the same hospital fighting for their life. While in the waiting room with the other families affected in separate auto/pedestrian accidents, we were able to grieve, encourage, and pray for each other. Their family member was a mother and fiancé. They had been out celebrating the holiday and their car was struck by a driver who the news says was potentially impaired. The driver, who had hit her, survived the accident and was taken to jail. Coincidentally he was my employee. I never told the family about the connection. Something inside me found it to be an irrelevant piece to the puzzle. Unfortunately, she didn't make it through the night and we never seen the family again.

This was definitely the most defining moment in my life, because everything that happened before it no longer mattered. My focus was now on Brazyl and being at the hospital every moment while she fought for her life. It was nearly 2 a.m. when things settled down. My wife and I remained in the room with Brazyl overnight. With the stress building as the night went on, Tiffany, who had stopped smoking a year prior, smoked nearly an entire pack of cigarettes, going in and out of the hospital most of the night. I just sat there listening to the beeps and watched the numbers on the monitors. There were three numbers that the nurses paid great attention to. One was her Blood pressure/heart rate, one was oxygen level, and the other measured the swelling of Brazyl's brain. I was hypnotized by those numbers. They were all that mattered to me, I accepted the fact that I was helpless. That there was absolutely nothing I could do for my baby girl except be there for her while she remained in a coma. I couldn't imagine being gone and receiving the call that she was no longer with us. I feared that conversation. I feared those emotions and feelings. I feared to live through the pain. I feared what we may have to go through the rest of our lives. And that fear took a toll on my body and my mind, and created a battle within. This was my first real experience of PTSD. Who knew I would gain so much from this painful experience.

2

GETTING THROUGH

Before starting this chapter, I would like to refer to chapter 1. To know more in-depth story about Brazyl's experience and recovery at the hospital, please purchase and read my wife's inspirational book From Tragedy to Testimony: A Family's Fight to Cope. In that book, she goes into detail about the experience from a mother's point of view, but this book is different. This is a story from my point of view, and the lessons I've learned through the pain.

When a person experiences tragedy, life immediately changes. Of course, the victim's life is affected the most, but the people who are close to that person are also affected, especially when that person is a child. In my case, my daughter was only six. She was so innocent and loving. I couldn't understand for the life of me why something like this could happen to a gentle soul like her? I am a true believer in karma and God. So, what negative act caused this experience to happen to us? Why do I have to feel this way? These are just a few thoughts that ran through my mind, and they appeared to arise quite frequently.

My wife was greatly affected by the accident. She became immediately depressed. Every day she wore the pain on her face. She cried so often, there was rarely a time that you did not see her face full of tears and with red puffy eyes. Although, she was trying to be strong, she was weak. The accident and the experience were beating her down. We would have many conversations, but they would end quickly due to her negative thinking. One conversation that stood out was when we were discussing Brazyl's future. While in the waiting room having lunch Tiffany was quiet thinking to herself and crying. I asked "What's wrong?" and she replied, "My baby was once a spunky and full of energy, vibrant little diva, and now what if she is a vegetable?" I would immediately interrupt and attempt to change her way of thinking. I knew that if we were going to get through this we needed to believe things would turn out realistically for the best, and realistically that is exactly what I believed.

For a man who had stopped praying much before the accident, I had begun praying all the time. Praying was giving me faith and a sense of relief. I was often talking to God, but never would hear anything in return. It honestly made me feel more hopeful and allowed me to get what I was feeling out of my heart. One of the main feelings that was bringing me down was resentment. Resentment of myself and actions leading up to this point. It was obvious to me that Brazyl had to have been paying for another's debt of karma, and the pain I was feeling I felt it had to be on us or me, I also resented God at a point. Although, I was praying, I was often upset and many of my conversations were sparked by questions of disgust like "How could you let this happen? If you God are real, why are we and all these people at this hospital feeling this pain?" Every day we were watching or hearing of someone dying. We would hear of something tragic happening on the news, then see the victim and their family at the hospital. In the room next to Brazyl's alone, we witnessed at least four or five deaths. That experience in itself causes trauma. When in the hospital, you hear everything that's going on around you if you just listen. We would often witness a new patient get admitted, and a day later the patient would be on life support with the organs being preserved to become a donor. It was obvious that was a crucial part of the business of hospitals. They would have a representative come to talk to the grieving family member and they would be very sympathetic and convincing at the same time. That instead of the body being laid to rest as no use to the future. Allow what's left of the body to save the lives of those waiting and in need. Although, I greatly respected the process, it wasn't a bridge I ever wanted to visit or cross, but the reality was that it was real and it was happening often. So, all I could and would constantly do is pray. Telling God how much I enjoyed Brazyl's presence in my life, and showed appreciation of her existence.

I felt completely bipolar. At one minute, I would be praying and hopeful, then something would trigger this feeling of hate and anger. The thought that would create these feelings were usually triggered by thinking of the driver. I used to think while my daughter is in this hospital fighting for her life daily— that the person who did this to her is running freely and -living his normal life hiding what he had done. These thoughts would cause me to fall into a severe depressive mood, because there was nothing I could do to get justice. I began to pray hurtful prayers against the suspect. I figured if anyone could get revenge it was God— especially after the way I was feeling.

The media triggered these feelings often. After a while, I became numb to it. We were doing interviews as much as possible. We were determined to have the suspect caught. We were calling on the community to step forward with any information they had regarding the suspect. We were also trying to flood the media with Brazyl's picture and story so that if the driver would see, the guilt would eat at him within. I wanted him to mentally suffer and get justice for Brazyl at the same time, but when the news would interview me and ask about the suspect. I would relay some bullshit positive message like we have forgiven him. We just want him to turn himself in. Knowing damn well if the police found the suspect, I would have done everything possible to seek justice of my own, and the fact that I couldn't was killing me.

With the story being on the news as frequent as it was, Crime Stoppers was being flooded with calls of leads regarding the case, but none were useful according to the detectives. I even had news anchors following up their own leads to me personally. Giving me addresses to possible locations of a car that had fit the description. I remember going to these apartments in the hood near Clark High School and finding a car that fit the description with the windshield shattered. When I saw the car I was fuming, I stood by the car until one of the neighbors came outside and asked about it as I was looking to purchase. After speaking with her regarding the car, she said it had not been moved for months. A dead end. I remember imagining what I would do if I found the person, which absolutely would have stripped me of my freedom. I was in the most unbearable amount of pain. When you are at a place of pain; many tend to not think of the consequences of your actions. The reaction is to get the feeling that you experienced out of you. I was in this place. All I could think about was justice for my precious baby girl that is fighting for her life. She should be home asleep in her bed and not in a coma.

Another instance had to be when I got a call that a car matching the description was parked at the hospital nearest to the accident site. I left not telling anyone and patrolled the parking lot till I found a car matching the description with damage to the front right bumper. I took pictures of the car, license plate, and stood by in the parking lot until security kicked me out. Then, I called the police to report and learn that the car was already reported and checked out by police and determined that it wasn't involved.

This was happening often, and to be honest, it was draining nearing exhausting. The feeling was full of adrenaline, like the feeling I would get when I was a police officer for a few years. Just five years after the experience I still had many of the training habits ingrained into my conscience. Hints the reason I was doing my own investigation. Regardless of what I knew or know, I had no business being there and needed to let the detectives and the police do their job, while I focused on Brazyl. This was evident to me as I noticed a pattern. I noticed that whenever I would leave the hospital to go on these investigations and return to the hospital, Brazyl would show a decline in improving. I paid attention to patterns as such, at the time just because of my belief in superstitions. This was developed from when I was younger playing sports. I would follow the clichés such as not stepping on the chalk line, not stepping on cracks, not splitting poles, not sweeping my feet, not opening the umbrella indoors, not walking under ladders. I also believed in lucky charms, lucky socks, lucky Frosted Flakes before the game, skipping rocks, making wishes on shooting stars, and my all-time favorite birthday wishes that always come true. I guess I always felt this sort of spiritual connection with the universe, and the many signs and symbols that I couldn't explain, so I kept it as a silent secret relationship that maybe only I understood. With that said, there was a pattern and from that action of going out, searching was bringing the negative result to myself and Brazyl. So, I definitely needed to stop, and focus on what's most important.

As Brazyl was getting better, Tiffany and I were getting worse. Each day became more stressful than the last, but we were determined to remain by her side. In the first couple of weeks, Tiffany and I never left the hospital to together. For the first week, we stayed at the hospital 7 days straight together. While family members kept our other children. Luckily, the hospital had a policy against this and started making one of us leave at night. This was difficult for us as we had supported each other through the pain. On day 8 I was on my own throughout the night. Alone, lonely, and empty. I needed something to do. The first night alone in my thoughts I decided it would be best to not think, so I stopped by Lee's discount liquor and bought a bottle of Honey Jack. As a pattern formed, I was drinking nearly a bottle a week. Drinking just to numb the pain and fall asleep. Tiffany was having the same problem, but was relying on cigarettes. She was not taking care of herself at all and fell into a deep depression. Three weeks into Brazyl's coma, we took it amongst ourselves to see our doctor. The doctor talked to us both and had us see a psychiatrist.

Not knowing much about therapy, we just picked the next available therapist. The psychiatrist meeting was us just telling the lady our pain and her recommending reading material. This was stupid to me because she provided no feedback, except handing us reading material to study and apply ourselves. This was an ineffective method for me as I hate to read. Not to mention, I could not even try to process any reading material the way my mind was thinking at that time. My pain wanted revenge. My pain wanted justice. My pain wanted my daughter to not lie in a coma suffering, which made my pain elevate to guilt. When I discussed this with the psychiatrist, she diagnosed us both with depression, anxiety, and PTSD. Gave us both Xanax and sleeping pills.

I was skeptical about taking the pills as the use of drugs for neurological reasons did not make sense to me. If I was sad and depressed, and the reason was valid then it was normal to feel that way, and I should learn to get through it. Tiffany on the other hand, desperately needed them to get through the trying time and pain she was experiencing. When she took them, I didn't notice a difference in her behavior. She seemed to me as her normal self, but then she would get tired and sleep for long periods. I remember when she would sleep all day. We would eat lunch and she would be asleep till the evening. It didn't bother me much, because she seemed so relaxed and peaceful while asleep. During that time, I would read to Brazyl and sing to her while she remained in a coma. At first, I was entertaining myself, but I noticed that when I was loud enough Brazyl's blood pressure and heart rate would elevate. It was as if she were conscious enough to hear me and understand and would get excited but was unable to express herself due to the medications. Once I discovered this and discussed via social media, someone donate a large bag of books. For hours throughout the day I would read with excitement and animation, and the more I was involved the higher her levels elevated. This mental stimulation was never studied by me, it was something that just worked. Once I learned that to be effective, I started looking into the music Brazyl loved before the accident.

She was infatuated with Disney Channel's Austin and Alley Star, Austin Moon. Austin was her little girl crush that no matter what she was doing, if he came across the TV or radio he got her undivided attention. She knew every lyric from the show. She knew every dance from the movies he starred in as well as his Disney music videos. Knowing this, I purchased the album on my phone, and throughout the day I would play it in the room next to her while as she laid in her medically induced coma. Not even heavy sedation could not stop her excitement as her levels would increase each time, she would hear a song. I played it so much that I began to learn it. Once I knew it, it was singing time. I would hold her hand and sing every song knowing she could hear me and feeling her joy. The nurses would walk in and I would just keep on singing. Although I was embarrassed, I was committed to Brazyl's entertainment, and I wanted her to know that I wanted her to live. I wanted her to know that I was by her side waiting for her to wake up. and when she woke up, if she didn't remember my face, she would always remember my voice. This is probably why when Brazyl woke from her coma her first word was singing songs. Neurologically, that was the only verbal patterns she could express, but that's another story. The lesson of this was to be conscious of patterns, good, and bad. Then be aware of the process and results of actions taken. With just a little bit of thought, you can leverage every situation.

3

COPING THROUGH

As Brazyl's healing body remains in a coma, I sit in the hospital recliner staring at the numbers on the machine. No worries as things are improving daily. She endured multiple lifesaving surgeries, which included a couple of scares. Brazyl was doing great. I, on the other hand, was decaying. The feeling of exhaustion had finally caught up with me. I stayed busy from early morning 4 am, lit on pre-workout caffeine or coffee once in the morning and again later in the afternoon. I hated the feeling of sluggishness. There was no way I could keep the little balance that remained in my life and rest like I needed. Plus, this was my way of battling the depression. I stayed busy, keeping things kosher at home and at the hospital. My days consisted of me getting the kids ready for school, dropping them off, and then straight to the hospital to be with Tiffany and Brazyl.

Tiffany and I would have breakfast. Breakfast time was the best time to communicate because the new day kept us hopeful. We both knew that Brazyl was getting better and things would be ok. We could now take this time to talk and examine each other. We would converse about anything, still able to flirt and tell jokes. It was a blessing to see her smile through the pain. It was more of a blessing knowing that we had each other to depend on. We both had our way of dealing with the time. These were our selected distractions. Mine was football and betting. I had so much time to study both college and pro, and with football on TV Sunday, Monday night, Thursday, and Saturday, I had plenty to read up on. Plus, the new William Hill app had just come out on the smartphones, and I was able to do all my sports betting from the palm of my hand. This was dangerously convenient, but it played a major role in my getting through the days. Tiffany's was reading. Her boss had dropped off at the hospital a care package and one of her best friends Amber dropped her off some reading material to pass time. In the box of books was a book called "Fifty Shades of Grey." She was stuck on this book reading throughout the day and then telling me about every chapter, which made conversations very interesting. Many of the stories had a way of turning you on and having these emotions during a time of pain made you want to f***. Not lovemaking, but f*cking. Within these erotic conversations with my wife, I had discovered my stress relief. "Pleasure through the Pain." Tiffany and I, at a time when we were younger had a wild sex life. We had more than a fair share of stories and are surrounded by closet freaky friends. We all know some crazy secrets about one another, and most friends are a phone call away. Tiffany had an acquaintance who was just the coolest and was into us. Although she was not my dating type, she had dope ass chemistry with us as a unit, and she was attractive with sex appeal. For privacy reasons, I will call her Natalie. Natalie and Tiffany had known each other for a couple of years at this point and in the past, she has played her role in a few of our fantasies. At this time, she was a true friend to Tiffany and was extremely supportive. She hated to see Tiffany sad and in pain, and was the type of friend that would do whatever to bring joy to the moment. Her song to us "Do what you want with my body." By Lady Gaga if I'm right. I'll Google it in a second... But as I continue this became a part of the healing process. Although, Tiffany had these new thoughts and fantasies, her PTSD and depression would not allow her to take her body to that level. Me on the other hand, I am a Scorpio with a firm belief in astrology, and if you know anything about Scorpios, we are freaks. I believe we are all in tuned differently. All my life, I have therapeutically used sex. Being married at a young age and not a drinker or smoker, my way to relieve stress, or celebrate was sex. Now, that I am older with experience, I have a better understanding of it psychologically. I have experienced the pros and cons of having such an addiction. As a boy, it created a weakness that my spirit was able to expose. The future content of this book will paint a picture of exactly what I mean. I feel by being transparent in that form will help others to identify whatever energy is holding them back from obtaining their greatness and with my wife's blessing and approval that will be my greatest intention.

After my Google search, it was Lady Gaga. Shout out to the artist and her spirit for creating that energy that brought me healing at a time of suffering. Natalie was truly inspired, and at this time I was listening to Ty Dolla$ign and Trey Songz, and all the songs were about threesomes. Music has a way of getting into your mind and creating a visual that your spirit begins to want to experience. Inspired by the art around me, and the cast willing, the scene was written and manifested in no time. My wife and I had been through so much, I believe she wanted to just see me happy and smiling. After being at the therapy place all day, and balancing life outside of Brazyl. Tiffany felt my depression and created a fantasy in her mind as well. Our not first experience, but first experience back at it. Tiffany was laid back about the experience. She said she just wanted to watch but wanted to be in control. I was hesitant at first, but I wasn't going to ruin the opportunity. I went along with it and played my part. Somehow, we had the house to ourselves. Just us three. I can't recall where the kids were, as time these times were hazy. But I know one thing for sure, we were able to create an epic experience.

Natalie came over dressed up, makeup, smelling good, and underneath matching sexy lingerie, and heals. She was all in. I was fresh out of the shower and comfortable, ready to perform. Tiffany was on some boss shit. In my opinion, is she was trying to find herself. She had been going through so much and when she cut her hair in solidarity for Brazyl, it took away a part of her. It was her sacrifice for Brazyl, and it was so powerful to me. This is when I learned the importance of self-identity and the struggles everyone faces through finding their confidence. This experience with Natalie was Tiffany's display of power and love for me. With the intention of healing and escaping a tough time, and it worked. Although, Tiffany didn't perform completely during the first time. The times following that were all magical.

So magical that it was apparent that the friendship had begun to shift. Tiffany and Natalie were talking on the phone a lot, and me being curious I always paid attention. Love comes with much energy. In the beginning, it can be good, but in the end, it can become destructive. Although, I was into Tiffany being in control of the situation, I was not going to be stupid. So, I began to create an energy that stayed involved. I begin to whisper things in her ear to make her think, but never overstepped my boundary in my opinion. I just made sure that she knew that I knew about them and their flirtatious past, and I was not going to be a fool. So, my play was just to make her our girlfriend. In that case, she could talk to her as much as she wanted without my worry. That also meant that she had to accept Natalie and I talking even when she was not involved, which came with the boundary of us not doing anything sexual alone. Based on the circumstance, it was appropriate, and all parties involved agreed. The perfect plan and I felt like a genius. To us, this was normal but semi taboo— it was a world away from our world. Plus, one of my best friends had a relationship similar, and he appeared to be on top of the world. Five years later, he is miserable, but that is another experience. Our experience once the title was placed was very short-lived. Me being an early morning person, I usually work out in the morning before 5 am. Because I was semi-active on social media at that time, I was posting my every movement. Not to show off, but to show my friends that I had not let the tragedy defeat me. To show them I was still driven. That I had hopes and dreams of a better future. That although times were difficult and painful, I still had every reason to live and love myself. And the messages were inspiring. Unlike Tiffany, Natalie was an early morning person as well and she would usually be my first like. Then, she started commenting, and then she was in my DM "direct messenger." Never was there anything that was sideways, just the usual morning introductions, such as a friendly good morning. And, how are you? Then, we would check each other's vibe and attempt to uplift or encourage. Then check each other's plans. Not much more exciting than that, but I was always checking the completeness of the union. At the time, our sex life was amazing, so I would let little stuff slide that rubbed me the wrong way about their communication and control of our relationship.

It was here that I learned the valuable lesson of the power of the healer. We all at some point in time experience pain and discomfort that create miserable moments that we feel will never end. Every minute feels like suffering as the negative thoughts run through our mind constantly feeling like a torture of the soul. We all also discover and practice different methods of coping with our pain— many of us do not even know how we are programmed. I have had to discover many methods of coping due to many unfortunate experiences, but in the end, I am stronger and wiser because of it. Every method (good or bad), has had me hooked. A feeling of euphoria, relief from pain and worry. A temporary happiness or escape from reality, which creates a condition of love that is powerful, but temporary. It's a feeling of appreciation and reciprocity.

What we had was special to me, but I noticed Tiffany's vibe towards it started to change. My first indication was the lack of frequency of intimacy. Now that we were all together, my ego started to flex, and I was bold in expressing when I wanted it. I was trying to be transparent and say how I felt. When it would not happen when I wanted it, I started to feel belittled, and I would get furious. It got to the point where I would literally crave it. My mind would visualize it, and it would consume my thought process. The thought of just seeing them two together would arouse me to the point that I felt like I was a sophomore in high school again. So did the thought of not being able to get what I wanted exactly when I wanted it, I felt like a little boy, and my ego was not having that. I was angry and bitter, and when Tiffany started saying things like "I'm not enough of a woman for you." That had me furious— One: because I loved her dearly. Two: because this was the Pandora's box that she had introduced me to as a young man early in our relationship and now I was accustomed to it. Three: because this was a decision we made together, it was bringing me joy, and now it was being threatened to be taken away from me.

Once this was established in my mind, all I would see is red and go back to a place of pain. These feelings would cause both of us to argue viciously. Word's feeling like a piercing dagger to the soul. They would get so bad that I would have to leave home and just go walk for hours at a time. Allowing myself to think— I learned this from a police officer back in my childhood days. When my mother and father would get into it and fight so bad that the police would have to come and keep the peace.

Back then, even if a battery had taken place, the woman had a choice on either to press charges or not. Many times, they would fight and when the police would come to the scene my mother would never press charges. The police officers got tired of wasting their time and I remember one telling my dad 'instead of hurting your wife every time you fight, why don't you take a walk instead...' This seemed to work well as the occurrences happened less with my parents. For me, it was then, and still is like meditation for me. Once I would begin walking, I would have this built-up anger and rage on the inside. As I walked, I would pay attention to my mind just go back and forth. Every thought was hateful and vicious. The voice in my head would be calling Tiffany all kinds of b*tches. Every flaw that I knew of her would run through my mind. The voice on the inside truly hated her for about 20 minutes. After running through those thoughts and vision of hate, I must say it was amazing how the mind full of negative emotions turned into something like a devil. This tricky mind with the intention of revenge is capable of anything. This energy became strategic and destructive, slow and methodical, but eventually careless. The way I was feeling was unappreciated, controlled, denied, oppressed, and revengeful. I knew what I had grown accustomed to, I knew what I wanted, and I would go at any lengths to get my thrill and make it meaningful. This, my friend, was the energy that destroyed my old self.

Although, Brazyl was home and getting better, I was falling apart and was miserable. I would leave the house daily feeling that negative energy, and most days I hesitated to return home. I felt so much guilt and resentment and just wanted to be away. It is amazing how energy works. One day, I was going through my social media and posted an update on Brazyl's progress. The public loved this because after being on the news multiple times, many began to follow Brazyl's story and looked forward to her progress. Many people would comment and give their inspiration, but this day, I received a notification from one of my exes named Lisa. She was a travel nurse and had been for many years. When she reached out it was very innocent and respectful. She asked about Brazyl and her injuries and how she was progressing. I was hesitant at first, but then she asked me a question that not many others who did not love me would ask, and that was, how was I doing and if I was remaining strong. She said she had been watching from the outside in and was proud of me. This sort of tone was needed at this time as I was down and insecure. Her words had a way of uplifting me and she was willing to listen.

This was a recipe for destruction. We began talking once or twice a week at first. Then, we began talking more, to the point we would be on the phone for hours. I would be neglecting work and taking along the way home. The way I began to feel, I was lucky she lived out of town. After creating a long-distance connection— things began to get routine. She would have a long drive home from work and would talk to me the entire time. Women have a way of making you reserve time and their attention. Especially, when both parties have their competition. A person that if you do not fulfill your role, there is another person in pursuit and waiting on the opportunity. This made me persistent. In the town she was living in, she talked about a corrections officer that was pursuing her, and she was taking it slow and getting to know him more. She said they met while at work and exchanged numbers and since we're getting to know one another. They had gone on a couple of dates, but never became intimate. Matter of fact, she said she hadn't had sex in two years. I was astonished knowing she had a strong sexual appetite. She said she was saving herself for someone she loved and respected. At first, I didn't believe her, but man was I curious. With that information, my mind was in full pursuit formulating a plan and opportunity at the next availability. She had family that lived in our town and came back to visit every so often. There was one time that she came into town to visit and asked me to come by. I visited her and we just went to this pool and talked for a couple of hours. We discussed our current life, our past relationship, our growth, our wins, our losses, and a bunch of other nonsense you talk about when you have not seen a person for so long. When you are a married man, women open up to you and tell you shit they won't even tell their closes friends. It's like a power of secrets and they trust you because you trust them, or else you wouldn't be talking to them. You would just talk to your wife— being able to get to know a woman on that level, you learn the way they think. You learn her strengths, weaknesses, priorities, morals, and history of experiences that make them the way they are, because they will fully open to you. You become a person of substance, guidance, a leader, and love begins to form. Not in love, but love like you love your favorite artist or song, because the art they create heals you and makes you feel connected. That energy that you can wait to experience, see, feel, hear. She was at that point, and I was just playing a fucking game. At this point, I was in it for the thrill. My life that I had created had fallen and broken into pieces. I was now wrecked and finding ways to make myself feel better. I was being sneaky, but not that sneaky. My wife wasn't paying attention to me. She was so focused on Brazyl and distracted by the United States of Entertainment, also known as social media, that I don't think she really cared after a while. Plus, she was dealing with her own anxiety battle, and I had got to the point where I stopped helping and being her support system. I stopped encouraging her, and just funded whatever venture or need she had. Looking back at it, I was giving my emotional support elsewhere, but also that was where it was reciprocated.

I was in a bipolar love triangle mess. As much as I knew, I should have shut shit down, I was looking forward to what would happen next.

"Self-destruction, you're headed for self-destruction."

4

Re"ZEN"tment

What the f*** have I gotten myself into? I was being evil. Straight evil with no regard or care of the consequences. I remember thinking to myself, what if I get caught? And the voice on the inside was like so what? If you get caught, how bad could it be? Tiffany would just leave, and you guys would split everything 50/50. You are not happy, your life is broken, and you will never be shit ever again. So, just have fun, live the best life you can out of the bullshit life you created.

I was dealing with some serious inner demons. I had become careless and completely selfish, but worse of all I hated my life and myself. This reminded me of a conversation my dad and I had as I was becoming a young man. I asked him about why he left us when I was a child. He answered, when my mother took away his dream of what he envisioned as a family, he created another family. He said after everything he had experienced and seen how my mother's philosophy on raising children was completely different from his, there would always be conflicts and issues. Which led to the frequent domestic violence occurrences, loss of freedom, and family torture.

I wasn't feeling this way, but I had started to understand it. It was the feeling of resentment. Resentment during marriage was a horrible feeling. This feeling changes the entire energy in the home. It also changes your intentions and connection with your partner and family. I had developed this identity on the inside that despised my wife. My anger and selfishness made me completely blind to what she was going through at the time. Looking back, she was at war with herself, and I was letting her fight the battle alone, due to my resentment. Emotionally, she had gone through so much over the past year and picked up a few bad habits. Bad habits that she had already fought to get rid of because they had caused problems in the past. She was back smoking, addicted to her phone and social media, eating unhealthy, anxiety so bad that she was literally stuck in the house afraid to leave, and not into anything I had going on. My resentment was finding every inadequacy about her. Some for good reason. Tiffany had shut down, becoming useless in many areas of our home and relationship. She was sleeping late, which made me responsible for getting the children ready and off to school. She wasn't cleaning house like she once did. No washing clothes or folding. She wasn't grocery shopping, running errands, or paying bills. Cooking was nearly nonexistent and had every excuse to not work out. She would just be doing her thing and taking care of Brazyl. The reason I know is because I was doing it all and I was exhausted every day. I could feel myself decaying within. At this point, I had many regrets and just wanted my escape.

Although, I wanted my escape, as I look at my situation, I never wanted to abandon my responsibilities or the family I created. What I wanted was a getaway— a chance to take a break from it and live another life, and with Lisa coming to town for her brother's birthday, she made it very clear the opportunity was open. When she announced she was coming to town, she let me know a month in advance. Our conversations became more frequent during the wait, full of flirtation and "what if's". I started spending long days at work acting as if I was always busy. I was creating a pattern of coming home late, so that when the time had come for me to be where I should not, it would not seem suspicious or out of the norm. Things at home were not changing much any. I was still coming home from work feeling miserable, and I was not doing anything to change the situation.

The day Lisa arrived in town, I noticed because her social media post of her landing at the airport. I figured I would play it cool and wait for her to contact me, and she did immediately. We spoke briefly and she had invited me to her brother's party, but I knew that I would look stupid there. Her family knew I was a married man, they knew what I had been through, and they knew me. How was I going to explain why my married ass was at this party? So, I declined. I told her to enjoy her family and would catch up with her another time. As she enjoyed her family, I chilled and kept my distance. Not calling or texting. The day after the party, she was at the brother's house, and I visited figuring this would probably be the only opportunity I would have to be away. As she opened the door and let me in, there they were, her whole family. Her mom, brother, sister, and us. Damn. While there, it was such a weird feeling to be welcomed and embraced. My conscience was vexed—they were asking me questions about my life that I was trying to escape from, and willing to lose. I was setting myself up for ultimate destruction. Looking back, I can envision myself following the road to the slaughterhouse. Walking into my own demise, at first not realizing, but eventually (2- hours later), my conscious got through to me and it was time to leave. When I made my rounds saying my goodbyes, I felt empowered in making the best decisions at the time. As I told Lisa I was leaving, she scurries to the as she tells her family she wanted to walk me to the car. I was like damn, I'm not out of this just yet. As we walked, we finally got to talk one on one for the first time of the night, since we had constantly been around family. Although she was slightly average looking, I knew I was always attracted to her physical confidence, vibe, and our connection. We had many similarities mixed with temptation and the forbidden. Tiffany and Lisa had a rocky past involving them going to blows because of me. Let's just say Lisa underestimated Tiffany due to their size difference, leaving Lisa with a face full of knots and a bruised ego. So much so that after the fight, and living with Lisa at the time, she checked herself into a hotel for 3 days to allow her face to heal. Fast forward to nearly a decade later, here we are. Here I am. Damn. After tossing around a few quick laughs, the conversation got emotional. Enough emotion to pause the conversation and lead to a passionate kiss. As we touched and rubbed, she somehow disengaged me, leaving us to go our separate ways. Although, I was leaving; I badly wanted to stay, but I needed to get home to my family before I destroy it. I got home maybe 11 or 12 that night. Tiffany didn't call and check on me or anything. When I got home everyone was asleep, leaving me to myself in my thoughts. I knew that what I was doing was wrong, but there was a part of me that didn't care. I knew what I wanted— I had already envisioned it and after all the time I had put into my efforts, I wasn't going to waste it. I was going to make it happen.

The next day I got the kids off to school and was off to work before Tiffany awakened. I worked diligently just in case I needed to leave early. Later that morning, I received a text from Lisa talking about the previous night and how bad she wanted us to see each other one last time before she left. It was a hot sunny scorching summer day in Las Vegas. She invited me to go swimming at her brother's High-rise pool. I agreed but needed some swim trunks for the occasion. I couldn't justify purchasing them, but lucky me I had my gym bag and in that bag was a pair of gym shorts I kept in the car just in case I ever wanted to stop and work out. I left work early and drove to the High-rise. We met at the pool and she had her sister and her sister's friend with her. Cool, we have company, What the hell? She sees no problem flaunting me around her family and friends? Oh well. I proceed to the shower room where I could change in privacy. While in the shower room the door opens, and Lisa walks in wearing a towel over her bathing suit. She locks the door behind her, and we create a scene that would be in one of those Tyler Perry movies. There was no turning back, I was committed to my decision. I was making my subconscious escape and being bad felt so fulfilling in the moment. After the fact, it was like once reality set in, I felt horrible. The whole drive home, the voice in my head was tearing me to pieces. "How could you risk it all for something so temporary? How could you leave your wife at home caring for herself and your disabled daughter? What if Tiffany did this to you?" These thoughts were constant. Internally, I was destroying myself. I knew I screwed up on a completely different level and I had no idea what to do next. I stopped answering my phone and calling Lisa. Talking to her caused too much confusion and I needed to get my mind right. That afternoon, I stopped by the park on the way home and sat there on a bench reflecting on my actions, and my life. I needed to make a decision. If I was going to continue to be reckless and jeopardize my family, then I needed to leave, but I couldn't leave. My family needed me now more than ever. I needed to step up to responsibilities and take control of my life. I needed to be a better husband and strengthen my wife everywhere that I saw weakness. I needed to create my happiness. I needed to be a much better man. I needed to change. I had become someone I despised. Someone with no heart, no emotion, and no self-control. What I was feeling temporarily had taken over me. I refused to let it become permanent.

When I arrived home, my family was there to greet me as if I were the greatest father ever. I looked into Tiffany's eyes and felt my deceit. I felt shame and evil. I walked into the bathroom looked in the mirror and felt hate for the asshole looking back at my reflection. I could not sleep that night when I went to bed. Thoughts were racing through my head constantly. I was realizing the differentiating voices guiding me in separate ways. I felt myself losing control of my life and giving up on everything I loved. I was completely dissecting and evaluating every aspect of life, trying to identify the areas of discomfort. Selfishness had me searching to find blame in everyone and everything but myself. When in all honesty, I was the only one to blame. I needed to change and desperately wanted to change, with no clue how and where to start. I sat on this thought for a few days, literally afraid to make my next move. Then I remembered a speech that was given to my college class by this Indian professor that was quite encouraging. He was inspirational and had many stories. During his speech, he used many references and the one that had always stood out to me was when he talked about the powers of the mind and mindfulness. He said that most thoughts are derived from the past or the future, and what we needed to focus on was now. He referenced and recommended a book by Eckhart Tolle called "The Power of Now." With his speech being so inspiring, I decided to purchase this book the same day. However, two years later, it merely became a mediocre decoration in my garage. So inspiring, yet I never bothered to read it. I found it in a spot tucked away, alongside my entire three-book libraries aside. I hated reading, but I knew that my answers were inside this book.

Something inside me was strongly gravitating towards the context. I opened it up and began my journey. I read every word, from the beginning dedications to the forward. During my reading, I couldn't concentrate though.

I had noticed that my thoughts were so strong that I was not comprehending. I was thinking about everything else except for what I was reading. This was alarming to me— I felt like I was mentally disabled. With no ability to focus, I had to figure out some new method to retrieve the information. I went on to YouTube and looked to find other methods of learning and the YouTuber had suggested listening to audiobooks. I searched for that title on YouTube and luckily someone had uploaded onto their channel and I began listening to it immediately. At first, I had a difficult time adjusting to the reader's tone cadence. The book was read by the author himself, and I had never communicated with a person who spoke as such. His vocabulary was different, but I had started to get used to it. The great thing about the audio book was the dialogue in between that helped to give understanding. It was like they knew what questions would be asked after hearing the chapter, and they had a great way of elaborating.

I was quickly gaining understanding. The day that was life-changing was the day I listened to the chapter on meditation. This was the day I gained my awareness. I was walking my dog and listening to the audio book daily for an hour. This day 20 minutes into our walk, we get to the part where Tolle is explaining his knowledge of meditation and bringing awareness to the body at first. Making the connection of the body to the mind and the signals they pass through. I paid attention to how the body connected with the mind through feeling and always gave forewarning of disorder through discomfort. I then paid attention to how these discomforts create barriers and limitations to our growth and advancement in this lifetime. What was pretty amazing was learning to feel the energy that was within. It was like discovering a new being that has always been there, but not paying any attention to it by ignoring it. The mind was in constant communication with, but I didn't notice. While in meditation I was attempting to communicate with it, but my mind would have so much chatter. My mind was thinking constantly. Tolle had said to try to silence the chatter, but the thoughts just kept coming. I would find myself not thinking of anything and then thinking about not thinking of anything. Then, I would get upset with myself for thinking too much, completely losing focus on wherever I believed I was headed. I would get to the point where I would pay attention to the thoughts. I would see how well structured they were. As well as the feelings, and emotions they created. How they took me into a dream in real-time. Where I could see and feel everything. I then paid attention to my breathing and began to take deep breaths at a slow count. Then, out of nowhere, I experienced a feeling of serenity. I was consciously unconscious and was in surrender mode. As I got deeper into my meditation, there was a moment where my mind asked: "Do you trust me?" I was confused. But as I proceeded the feeling, breathing got more intense and before I completely surrendered, I got afraid and opened my eyes. I was amazed. "Did I really just meditate, or did I just take a quick nap?" I said out loud. No, I meditated. I remembered everything I was thinking and felt like I was experiencing. My heart was beating fast and I was semi hyperventilating. I felt it. It was an amazing eye-opening discovery for me that allowed me to tap in and think on a new level. A level of knowledge and discipline. The euphoria I had been desperately looking for.

With knowledge and discipline, any human being can be powerful. But first, you need mind control, and this is what I learned from my experience of Tolle's teachings. As I got furthered into my experiences with meditation, I learned that whatever is going on in your life at the time greatly influences your thinking, meaning that if the energy surrounding you is positive, then the majority of your thoughts are of gratitude and finding ways to keep that joy. The mind will give you thoughts of moments of the past and allow you to relive that moment, feeling the same emotions and feelings that are attached to the memory. I quickly realized that my way of thinking was causing my depression, resentment, and anger. Always thinking of the past and the misfortunes, never thinking of the blessings or acknowledgements. If I thought about the accident, I would experience emotional pain and sadness. Those thoughts would cause me to protect my ego and become angry. My anger would cause me to abandon all thoughts of joy and happiness and now look to lash out or find some way to suppress my feelings before I did or said something I shouldn't. Usually, I would take to listening to some aggressive type of music, watching fights on World Star, or just having an unapproachable attitude. These feelings transforming me into a person that

I genuinely was not.

As I got deeper into the practice of meditation and paying attention to my thoughts and feelings, I was able to discover my go-to vices for discomfort were either sex or sweets. Both had always been my kryptonite and I never questioned why. It seemed the mind had a pattern, and if it wanted immediate satisfaction that was my play. There had been many experiences in the past where I used both to abandon an emotional feeling and call it relieving stress— but I never understood how strong the mind was at creating the illusion until this breakthrough experience of meditating. While in meditation, everything was as normal, but I kept having these visions of Tiffany wearing one of my tee shirts that covered her seductively, allowing just a peek of her hips to show if she were to bend over. I knew that's what she went to sleep wearing the night before with no panties. As the vision appeared in my meditation my body began to react. Just the mere thought of sex got me aroused. I then tried to abandon the thought by letting another arrive, and I immediately felt my body become in a relaxed normal state. This was where I stated to learn that the world, I was creating all started in my mind. This was a breakthrough for me because it made me become conscious of my thinking. During meditation, I developed the ability to recognize a thought and how that thought made me feel. If the thought did not benefit my "Now," I learned to let it go, and allow another to arise. This prevented me from getting wrapped up in thought and creating or replaying a scenario, and how I could have said or done something differently. As well as revisiting old emotions and wasting a tremendous amount of time. This skill also allowed me to realize that I had time to shift my way of thinking before acting out of emotion when feeling angry, hurt, or defensive. You start to realize the people around you, who have no control of themselves, and triggers that antagonize others to lose control. Certain phrases, memories, actions cause people to get into their emotions, and completely flip— or you notice this in yourself. These are the things that the mirror does not show but must be discovered and overcome. These are the thoughts that have the ability to live in your mind forevermore and create strong influence.

It became apparent to me that my mind had taken control of my life and I was allowing my life to continue on its downward spiral. Once I was aware that things could change, all I needed to do was change my mindset. I began to acknowledge all the flaws that I had discovered and focused first on getting control of the mind. Once I was able to tame it, who knew what I was capable of? I was determined to discover this. I had finally identified the voice within that would appear when I was trying to read, distracting me from comprehension, and handicapping my learning ability— or the voice that would appear when running or working out. Saying, "Stop, why you are even enduring this pain." Or the voice that told me, "I want ice cream and I need it now." Or the voice causing me this anger— I also discovered this encouraging voice that told me that I could do anything, and that change started with me. I needed motivation, but I needed something new. That's when I searched on YouTube and discovered for my first time the great Les Brown. This dude spoke fire into my soul. He made me want to do better and his philosophy and stories gave me an understanding of myself and the people around me. He made me think strongly of my purpose and my gifts, and made me believe that "It ain't over," and that God has a purpose for me and my life. With this attitude, it might sound fleshy, but I felt like I had been reborn. I was hungry and ready to take on the world, or was I?

5

REBORN

As the year 2014 was wrapping up, just like every other end of the year, I performed a self-audit to reflect on my life and discover what direction I was headed in my future. I was very proud of myself for changing the narrative of my decisions and keeping the pieces together of a life that had been shattered and turned upside down. Not just for me, but my entire family had experienced the worst pain of our lives, and we stuck together through it all. Brazyl was making progress daily, constantly giving us something to celebrate.

Her recovery was going amazing. So amazing that she was released from Care meridian Rehabilitation in March of 2014 and had returned home to experience life at home under new conditions where she would receive at home therapy and homeschooling. This was a big change for me, because Tiffany and I would spend all day at the facility while Brandon Jr. was at school and Berlyn was at daycare. I was exhausting myself these days, especially the days I slept at the facility, which was three to four times a week as Tiffany and I would switch off every other night. That was one of the reasons we chose Care meridian as they allowed one of us to stay with Brazyl. She had her own room and an assigned nurse— the rooms were of a nice size and comfortable even with the gurney sitting in the middle. They allowed us to decorate the room and we did so with one of Brazyl's favorite, Hello Kitty. There was hello kitty everywhere from her comforter, to stickers on

THE PAIN OF A MAN

the walls, and her trash can. This was in light of the community figuring out about her interest of Hello Kitty and the gifts kept pouring in. There would be Hello Kitty toys, stuffed animals, posters, necklaces, and anything you could imagine. It was as if people would see Hello Kitty and think of Brazyl, and then buy it for her. They would then send the gifts to the facility. She always received gifts and fan mail. The community was very in tuned to her recovery and with it going so well, she was always reaching a milestone quite quickly. We would post about it on her Facebook fan page, and every news outlet would want to cover the story. This had not been like anything I've ever experienced or seen. It was apparent that in our big city she was popular. How couldn't she be though, she was so amazingly strong, and her fight was inspiring. The media loved our entire family— we were strong, we had faith, we remained positive, and we were persevering.

Brazyl motivated me like no other. Her fight to live gave me the energy to overcome and stay strong as well. The nights I would stay with Brazyl the nurse always come in the room around 4 am. That's when I would wake up and hit the gym for a two-hour workout session. This would be a solid two hours as I would become numb to the pain beating myself to relieve the inner guilt. I would go to the gym with my earphone, hoodie over my head, and zone out. Not even making an eye contact with anyone in my entire workout session. I was focused, only thinking about myself and the pain and grimace on Brazyl's face, when she would be working in rehab. That vision alone could get extra reps when the muscles were exhausted. The tears that would come down her face from her eyes as she had difficulty strengthening her weak frail muscles, but never giving up. I used that energy to fuel my every workout, and it provided an edge that I wasn't used to. I developed a routine and a new passion. Working out had become my escape and was therapeutic. I was gaining confidence with every workout and feeling better about the future.

Although I was feeling better, Tiffany was still struggling to find herself. She had begun writing her book but got distracted with her new venture selling adult toys as an independent contractor for Passion Parties. I supported her in this venture because it would challenge her on the things that she was battling within. Before Passion Parties, Tiffany never went anywhere and wanted to do nothing due to her anxieties. This allowed her to become razor-sharp focused on the venture. She would spend two to three hours studying the product and their use. Being great at sales, this was a great opportunity. What was even better was that she got to get oils, lotions, and toys for ourselves which was an amazing experience as it really spiced up our sex life. My favorite was the vibrating ring and she enjoyed the vibrating Insert that I controlled from an app on my phone. I was falling in love again and was destined to get Tiffany's confidence up as she was reshaping her identity. She began to get her hair styled in many different hairstyles as with short hair, she was able to be more creative with her way of expression.

As she was coming back into herself, I began to see an awakening in Tiffany, but noticed she wasn't inspired to write the book she had begun months prior. She had a lot of free time on her hands and one thing I had learned during my studies of motivation and overcoming depression was that your dreams have the power to awaken you. Meaning that whatever it is that you desire can manifest perfectly through your pain. Bringing a greater level of fulfillment and achievement. I simply had her identify her goal and told her she could not fail at this. I knew the words resonated with her because she sat there quietly. The next day, she was back to writing and focused on the pursuit of her goal. It was an amazing experience to witness, I had seen her focused before, but never on this level of focus. She knew what she wanted, and I was going to make sure that I supported her. I made sure that when I was home, I took care of all responsibilities and duties, and limited distractions. This allowed her freedom to be able to write and the further she got in the process; the longer she would write. She would be writing from the time the children went to bed till the early AM. We weren't spending much time together, but we were there for each other. I used my free time to work on me and rest. Constantly working on my ego, mindset, and anger. The teachings were working as I was constantly in the now and no longer feeling any resentment.

I felt myself growing and gaining control of myself more and more each day. Once I identified my weaknesses and began to work on them, I was on the road to being a better man. I became more patient, focused, and was able to control my thoughts. Which allowed me to become a much better comprehending reader. Reading increased my vocabulary and I could feel myself becoming smarter and wiser. I began to dive deeper into my reading, reading books like "Man's Search of Meaning" by Victor Frankal, "The Seat of the Soul" by Gary Zucov, Tao Te Ching, amongst many others. These books were giving me a new understanding of life.

Going into 2015, I had completely put 2014 behind me. Although I was content, I still was not happy. But I determined to create happiness. As the year began, I turned on YouTube and searched for motivational videos. There were many videos, but only a few stood out. One in particular was a compilation of speakers and there was one speaker who I later researched and found out who was Les Brown. This man's message was heaven sent and perfectly placed there for me to find at the right time. Every sentence this man spoke resonated with my soul. His words were everything that I needed to hear to find the encouragement in myself that I was awaiting someone else to provide. In my reality, no one was coming— no matter how bad I needed it. I was going to have to get myself back on track. Just that thought alone was enough to shift my mindset.

With a new mind and Les Brown speaking life into my soul, my entire approach to life had shifted. I had now become mindful of every aspect of my life and held myself accountable for what had resulted thus far. This approach allowed me to be focused on the present moment and search deep within, discovering my strengths and purpose. Tiffany one day was having a discussion and she mentioned to me something about public speaking and joining a group called Toastmasters. I dragged my feet on the idea, but the seed was planted. Before I could focus on me though, I wanted to put my focus into every area of my life that was causing discomfort. One was my relationship with my wife. I felt like I owed her so much, especially for all that we had been through, and the guilt I felt for the wrong I had done. I was determined to create happiness and said yes to everything. One of her goals was to go on a cruise, I was excited because I too wanted to go on what would be our first cruise. During our childhood, we both had never been, and who would be better to share the moment with? We booked the tickets in January for March. The wait seemed like nothing as we anticipated Valentine's Day. This was the year I would go all out. I wanted Tiffany to feel spoiled. I went on an internet shopping spree buying her everything I loved that I know she would love. I bought her 2 pairs of MK high heels, a sexy red pair, and a black pair. I couldn't decide which one I liked more. Two dresses, perfume, a gel nail LED kit, and all the gel polishes, plus more. She was extremely happy and reciprocated the love.

Leading up to March, I started to train excessively with the intent to get my body in shape for the cruise. I was spending a lot of time away from home as I was at the gym. This was causing a disconnect in our relationship, and being aware of that energy, I was searching for a solution. I came across this ad selling an entire gym worth equipment on craigslist for a very low price. I responded to the ad and met the guy at the storage facility, and when I got there, the equipment was looked better than it had in the pictures. I made the purchase, got a U-Haul, drove home, and created my own gym in my garage. I had everything I needed, plus I was right there at home, just a yell away. I fell in love with the garage staying there five to six hours a day. I would work out at least four hours a day. I would read, meditate, and chill there daily. It had become my sanctuary. Although, the children and Tiffany would often interrupt me, I didn't mind it at all. I liked that they got to see me working hard on myself and becoming alive.

It's crazy what you can accomplish with a vision and determination. My body was changing rapidly. Results were instant and my discipline was like no other. In just two months, I was in the best shape of my life and I looked amazing. As we got closer to the cruise date, I started experiencing some depression. As I was checking on our funds, it caught me by surprise that we had spent so much money in such a short time. Our financial cushion was gone, and we still needed to fund our time on the cruise. The last thing I wanted to do was go on vacation on a budget. That would take the fun out of the experience, but I also didn't want to come home broke. Back to living paycheck to paycheck. Living like that, for me as a man is one of the absolute worst feelings on this earth. I can think of worse feelings, but paycheck to paycheck is mental and physical slavery. Life with limits sucks when so many people are living happily, what appears to be worry-free lives. I think much different now, but at that time my mind was ignorant and immature, and allowed thoughts to sabotage me.

The day before the cruise I decided to have the best time possible and deal with real-life when I returned home. I didn't have to worry about my kids, as our good friends, Kristine and her husband Richard agreed to stay at our home with children while we were on vacation. I highly recommend this, especially if you have pets and kids. In this way, the children can be comfortable being themselves in their own way in the environment, damaging their own things and eating their own food. Same with the pets, they can stay home in their own environment and not have to be in a kennel. This also allowed my son BJ to feed the dogs, so I didn't have to worry about any incidents involving my dog and the other kids. Everything was in place. At that point, I just needed to get my mind right. The day before the cruise, I woke up early that morning around 4 am, before the rest of the family awakened. I got deep into thought and prayer and meditated for an hour. This was nearly a record for me, but during that time I experienced a breakthrough. Everything was normal at first, but as I continued to focus on my breathing, I felt myself as I surrender. The best way to describe my experience was I trusted myself not to die. I came to the realization that my body would sustain life itself as long as I followed the commands of the mind and its triggers. I learned that I didn't control 100% of myself, but there are a universal connection and essence with every breath. As I surrendered and remained awake, my body naturally sustained itself. Although, I felt like if I stopped controlling my breaths I would stop breathing. I again surrendered in fear and eventually, I felt the experience of nirvana. Knowing that made me feel more alive and appreciative of my existence. I gained consciousness and woke with an entirely new perspective. The best part was that I was able to put the past behind me and focus on every moment that I would experience and try to participate in it to its entirety.

As we drove to California, Tiffany's father decided to drop us off. Allowing me to think and rest on the way there. Being able to control your thoughts gives you a pleasure and brings value to your thinking. Uninterrupted thinking is one of the best times ever. I tried to pay attention to all my thoughts. If I could remember them, I tried to recall what triggered that thought and manifested that feeling. The thoughts during the drive were all joy— I just wanted to have fun, but most of all, I wanted to see my wife enjoy herself.

Once we got on the boat, all worries arrived, but after we left the dock, we went to the bar and got a drink. About an hour later, we walked out onto the dock and all you could see is a never-ending ocean. The ocean was so massive, and my mind realized that I was just one soul on this massive planet in a much massive universe. Until then, I was so much more important, and my mind was individualized, which made me huge. Now, I was feeling like I was a part of the whole existence and only responsible for my part that I have created or that has been given to me. This was an emotional time of my life and definitely helped me transition, and when I looked to my side to see that the woman that I love standing right next to me. I would conclude that I would fulfill every role needed as a husband in order to support her destiny.

The remainder of the cruise was a great time. We got to experience things that we only could imagine and more. Not being heavy drinkers, we spent our money on experiences. We went to comedy shows, played bingo, wine tasting, eating, took a land tour, went shopping, and took advantage of the ships entire daily schedule. One thing I've always loved about our marriage is our ability to have fun once we are in the environment. Tiffany knows how to have a good time, especially when she is happy, and we had an amazing time. I was watching her come alive. This showed me that these were the type of moments that need to be experienced and repeated with new destinations, being shared with loved ones often. Experiences like this gives life new meaning and enjoyment. Something to aim for, capture, and tell stories about. We had a great time and felt an incredible amount of release. Being on the ocean so long, not talking to the children or being on social media brought on some anxiety. So, there came a point where we couldn't wait to get home. The drive back home was comforting— very reflecting and allowed us to discuss our goals moving forward. I needed to find a new venture and a new goal for myself.

The last few years had just been about surviving and healing. I was ready to start living again. Tiffany was focused on her book and getting it published. We knew nothing on how to make this happen, but somehow, we would figure it out. Once we arrived home it was back to reality. We were focused now more than ever. Vacation opens your mind in ways that create possibilities. It shows you that there is more to life and much more for the mind to experience. Vacation takes away limited vision. It disconnects the mind from the programming, as you can witness the many different lifestyles and people. There are people out here living that life. People that are constantly enjoying life, but most importantly creating experiences. We met people who travel every other month living their best life, because they were able to do so. "Now, to come to think of it theoretically, maybe they are just trying to get away from their life? Maybe their version of reality is prosperous, but unhappy and miserable. On the other hand, maybe they accomplished their dreams and goals and now would like to celebrate. Whatever it may be, I want to live a life with the ability to do so if I choose without limitations on my mind. This was my motivation and now the only question was, how?

I was focused on my family, providing, and caring for them, but also working on my confidence and mentally preparing myself for the future. Tiffany was focused on her book and would achieve her goal of finishing her project. I've always admired this about her. Her ability to create and manifest her vision. She had captured our entire experience from her point of view in an inspiring way, plus she had created so many relationships in the media from Brazyl's situation that she had the local support and publicity needed to market herself. The process of finding a publisher was new to us. This was the most difficult part of the process. No deals were satisfying enough to Tiffany, so she decided to self-publish after a friend referred her to a self- publishing company. We had no money to invest at the time, but I was determined to find a way. I tried many ways that fell short. Tiffany seemed to worry that we wouldn't get it published after she had poured her heart out into the project.

I couldn't let her down. The thought of her disappointment pushed me to find a solution. So, I took out a loan and invested in the publishing and buying 1000 books. The shipping and handling alone was $1200, but I was excited to support her dreams. Plus, I truly believed in her success. Once we placed the order we waited for a month or two. In the meantime, I was continuing to work on myself and advance spiritually and in knowledge. I had begun to study success and many of the books I was reading had mentioned public speaking as one of the main skills that needs to be improved upon. Remembering my wife planted the seed about Toastmasters in my head, but when Les Brown and Zig Ziglar said it, I knew I needed to take action. I researched the Toastmasters here in Las Vegas and nearly 500 clubs popped up. All differentiated by time, dates, experiences, and niche. I choose a Monday afternoon club called Holistic Toastmasters. In the picture, there was two black men and one black woman. The rest of the group was very diverse, but like most clubs predominantly white. It seemed like the perfect spiritual group to connect with and my first visit took place July 5th, 2015. When I arrived, everyone was extra friendly, and their welcome blew me away. Every member participated in my greeting and their role in setting up the room for the meeting. I was made comfortable immediately, but that all changed when I was asked to introduce myself during visitor. I followed with the driest, most boring intro ever, nervously saying, "Hi! My name is Brandon Ward, from Las Vegas," and proceeded to sit back down. Once I sat down, the entire room of 15 members caught me by surprise and gave me an applause. That applause felt amazing! Although, it was a part of the culture, it made me feel like "I belonged there," and I would crave for the applause from that day onwards.

6

BECOMING THE SPEAKER

When you crave for an applause, there is no better place to be than in a Toastmasters meeting.

Toastmasters International is a non-profit educational organization that teaches public speaking and leadership skills through a worldwide network of clubs. Headquartered in Englewood, Colo., the organization's membership exceeds 357,000 in more than 16,600 clubs in 143 countries. Since 1924, Toastmasters International has helped people from diverse backgrounds become more confident speakers, communicators, and leaders.

With that said, every time you speak according to your role, nearly every member will clap. This became part of my motivation to speak. Not just for the applause, but for the result that my words brought to the universe through me. I now had the ability to develop the skills needed to deliver my message to the world supported by a platform to deliver it. When asked if I would be participating in the meeting or just observing, I agreed to take part although I was nervous.

This was a weird, yet enlightening experience for me, because as a person who meditates, I feel like the world is slowed down for me. I paid attention to every thought in my mind and every feeling in my body. Eckhart Tolle would describe this feeling as "The Watcher". I am connected to the entire experience, constantly learning something about my conscience, but not allowing it to make my decisions. As the meeting went on, I felt myself becoming more and more anxious, but seeing other people wear their emotions and fight through it that made me feel more comfortable. I admired the bravery of the novice and the skill of the experienced. My ego was destined to see where we sat on the scale and would find out during Table Topics. Table topics is where you had a minute and a half to discuss a random topic chosen by the Table Topics Master, and today's theme was Independence Day. One member went up and discussed independence. Another went up and talked about the American flag. One lady who was an animal activist talked about animal torture inhumane practices. Then the Table Topics Master called my name, and said what does the Fourth of July mean to you? As I got up, I took my time and strolled to the front of the room. My mind immediately was searching for a story and an analogy. I had been listening to motivational tapes majority of the following week, so I knew my intentions. After shaking the TTM's hand the story setting came to me. I saw a firework stand and came up with a minute and twenty-second speech about how every firework in the stand is different and represent us as people. I spoke about how we all just need that one spark (Inspiration), which creates a flame (Motivation) that lights our wick, which provides us with an opportunity to show our creative beauty for the world to see. This talk got me not just a round of applause, but a standing ovation. Surprisingly at the end, I won the competition and got a ribbon. I love those ribbons... I was hyped up, proud of myself, and confident. I was extremely surprised how all the nervousness disappeared after I spoke my first sentence. Internally, I was breaking barriers that were created by fear in the mind. Following the meeting, I was embraced and of course, encouraged to join the group. I needed no sales pitch and agreed immediately. Feeling as if this was an assignment on my destiny, and being that this was a holistic group, it was just what I needed. I easily could have chosen a group of people who looked just like me, but I was trying to learn as much as I could during the experience, and this was the most diverse group of people I had ever seen. In the past, old white people made me feel uncomfortable. An early experience in life has always had me on guard when around them. I felt as if they believe they are here on earth to judge, but do not understand what they are looking at or care to even learn. This is something I needed to get over, because honestly, I was the one who was judging, although there was no malice on my part just observation. I think of this scenario much different now while writing this, but at the time of this story, this was my way of thinking. Either way, whatever I was looking to get out of the scenario was received as I move forward. Anyhow, in this group was three or four people, and they were amazing and supportive. The group consisted of many people in the holistic niche, yet none of us were alike. We had young, middle-aged, and older— male, female, gay, straight, and a mixture of ethnicities. This was the perfect place to plant myself and grow, and that's exactly what I did.

Volunteering to speak at every chance I could. I choose to give my ice breaker (First Speech) the following week. Ecstatic, I went home following the speech to share the experience with my wife. She listened and embraced my excitement— I thanked her for the idea and asked for her support. A new dream had been birthed; I would become a professional motivational/inspirational speaker in the footsteps of Les Brown.

Knowing I had a week to work on my first seven-minute speech, I wasn't aware of the anxiety this caused. I felt a new pressure but could compare it to my days of playing football, where we practiced all week for our games on Fridays or the weekend. Practice, prepare, practice, prepare, rest, and execute. This was repetitious, but a formula that I was used to and could formulate into my new endeavor. My only problem is that I didn't know what to talk about. What were my intentions? What did I want them to know? What did I want them to take from it? I was drawing blanks. What was my inspiration? Two days passed and still nothing. Until one day the kids were teaching each other a dance they learned called the moonwalk, which was mastered by the legendary Michael Jackson. The kids were watching his videos on YouTube and came across "The Man in the Mirror." I had seen the video before, but never as an adult. The song itself is great and inspiring, but to I captured its meaning. The video tells a story that raises awareness of the problems in the world, and the way we change it is to start with the man in the mirror, meaning ourselves. This resonated with me, because as I looked in the mirror, there was so much I needed to change and learn. I felt ignorant, and Jim Rohn said, "The worst thing you could be is stupid, unintelligent, and uninformed." It is then, when the world will take advantage of you, and there is nothing an ignorant person will do about it. I set off even more destined to learn, but first I had to write the speech. After sitting in meditation, the ideas began to flow and in no time, I knew my speech and it was good. I would use props, tonality, and engage the audience. When the next meeting came around, I was confident. Speaking against me that day was to me; one of the best speakers in the group James. James was very intelligent. An articulate, and focused speaker. It was clear that he was on the mission to get better and he seemed seasoned. At Holistic Toastmasters, every week the speakers are in a friendly competition that gets voted for the best speech by the attending members. James went first, killing it as always. His speech was as close to perfection as one can get. I admired his style and his use of large intelligent vocabulary words. After he spoke, he received a great ovation. The joy could be heard as the other members of the group singing his praise. Rightfully so, as he deserved it, he was great. This shifted my confidence. How the heck was I going to follow this perfect ass speech? The Toastmaster for the day took back over the lantern, again giving James his props and praise. He then turned his attention to me. My evaluator touched on my agenda for the speech and then the Toastmaster introduced me saying, "Looking for to what this young man has to say. New to Toastmasters and presenting his ice breaker speech titled "The Man in the Mirror." I walked up feeling the pressure and nervousness, but once I started all those feeling turned into a passion. I felt every word and the emotion behind it. I was confident, loud, animated, and yelled at myself as I looked into the mirror prop having a dialog. The dialog was real, and I was really into with myself. Telling myself my flaws, my inadequacies, and my weaknesses. I then followed up by encouraging myself. Telling myself affirmations and reminding the man in the mirror what I had experienced and how I persevered. The audience eyes were glued on me with watery glares and stares. When I got done, they damn near erupted in the room. The applause was so fulfilling to my soul. When I sat down, as the feeling of complete joy came over me, I was thoroughly exhausted. I felt like I had just sprinted a few miles as the sweat soiled my undergarments. I poured my heart out, and never had I experienced that feeling or emotion— I felt full. Like I was on my mission and gave my best. The group tallied the votes, and in the end, I received more and was victorious— this was an instant boost to my confidence. Now, I understand why they say embrace the many goals on the way to the big goal, because the joy is in the experience. This was the path of my journey and I knew I was where I was supposed to be.

Feeling motivated and full of ideas from my many hours of reading books on psychology, spirituality, philosophy, and speaking. Finding content to speak about became simple, but the issue was having too many ideas. I still volunteered to speak again at the next meeting. I wrote and delivered a speech title "Your Gifts, Your Path, Your Purpose." This speech was about developing your God-given gifts and talents, placing them on your path in route to your destiny, and serving your purpose. I discussed the pitfalls of chasing dreams despite being undisciplined and unknowledgeable, also the challenges along the path and how they exist to sharpen us and promote us to the next level of our endeavors. As a new member of this group, my intention was to make a name for myself. This philosophy came from a motivational speech I heard regarding self-image. I believe it was Zig Ziglar that said during his speech that you must create a vision of who you want to become and work every day and every moment becoming that. Becoming who you want to become is based on the decisions and actions and amount of effort. My goal was to make others believe in me so that I would believe in myself, and I would do so by my work ethic. This was a new commitment for me added to my many others, but I was with it because I needed a new journey badly. Life had become a rat race for me. I felt like going nowhere and needed some adrenaline of the mind, and speaking was my way of getting it. The emotions and adrenaline I feel in front of a crowd, even if it's just 10 people, is rich in the moment. At that point and time, I feel so vulnerable but so powerful. When you're new to it; you're full of emotions, but constantly hearing voices in your head. The spotlight is on you and you're the star of the show. People's time and attention are dedicated to you, and you better be dedicated to them. I was dedicated and following the philosophy of the best, Les Brown.

Prior to the meeting and me presenting my speech we acknowledged our guest in attendance. There were two women visiting from a sister Toastmasters club. Sharon and I forgot the others name. Sharon introduced herself as one of the leaders in our division and was there to observe and not participate. I felt even more pressure, but just like sports, I was up to the challenge.

When it was my turn to speak all eyes and attention was on me. I was once again nervous, but when I said the introduction, which was delivered in a scripted way based on the way I heard everyone who was experienced in public speaking begin their speech— which was a basic "Good morning fellow Toastmasters and welcomed guest," and immediately the nerves surpassed. I delivered this talk with all the passion I could. While speaking I noticed Sharon deeply engaged nodding her head at every point and never really blinking. As I wrapped up the speech, I received great applause and won another speech competition achieving the blue ribbon. Following the speech, Sharon approached me saying how much she enjoyed my talk, and how my message would be great for the students of Clark County. We exchanged information and later that evening she emailed me, putting me in touch with a guy in charge of connecting speakers with the schools. After exchanging a few messages, I was invited to speak the following week at a middle school in Las Vegas for a program called PAYBAC.

PAYBAC is a program created to put community leaders in contact with students, with the intent to encourage education and achievement. This program makes 3040 appearances yearly at schools throughout the valley and has been established for over two decades. My first speech was in front of an eighth-grade science class. I arrived wearing my signature look a business suit, tie, leather gator Stacy Adam's, and a YIAM snap-back hat. This look has always appealed to me, as it is the same look that the NFL draft recruits wear after the announcement of their new team. Plus, I have a big head, and no one need to see all that. The children loved the look, and I managed to stand out amongst my peers. Many children thought I was a pro athlete and asked what team I played for. I told them I was no pro, but I will always be an athlete. I will always be in shape because I am constantly trying to get better.

After having this discussion, it became apparent that I needed to include this in my speech. Although, they have heard about health in many classes. Sometimes we just need to hear from someone who can deliver the message and inspire the action. As men, we have been conditioned to be told what to do and await approval of those above us on this hierarchy system that has been created, with some of us coming to a breaking point where we rebel and believe we can do it all on our own. Only seeking a new master with new inspiration. Now and then a messenger arrives, awakening you to the possibilities that exist in you. But only if you make a few life adjustments. As we talked more about health, the kid asked about my career as an athlete. I have seen this as another learning experience. I am ready to tell this class my story.

Before telling my story, I asked the class to share what their dream is. Many had great answers such as becoming a veterinarian, lawyer, doctor, military serviceman, officer, firefighter, famous YouTuber, and in low-income areas many want to become pro athletes. I began this story saying, when I was younger my dream was to be a professional baseball player. Growing up playing in little league I was amazing amongst my peers in Southern California, Rialto to be exact, was my stomping grounds. Baseball was my life, my love, my everything. Every year from the time I was five years old, I constantly got better. My father taught me the importance of work ethic and getting better. Just the distraction I needed from home life— I played baseball daily. Even just for a fun time with my friends in the neighborhood. We would make balls out of newspaper and tape. We would even paint a square on the wooden garage and play strikeout. The bend on those curve-balls were ridiculous. We would play home-run derby with pine cones, whiffle balls, bottle caps, anything we could get our hands-on. This love for baseball consumed my life, and no one could tell me I wasn't going pro. Baseball developed my reputation and got me my respect. Constantly winning and constantly clutch. When your clutch everyone loves you. Clutch people create life's greatest moments— bringing joy to everyone connected except for the adversity, but even though they respected the competition and effort. I was always clutch, and I was always consistent. To me, my entire career was filled with ESPN top play moments. As for hitting, I was always at the top on batting average and home runs. Going through the years, my mind was only set to go pro until I got into high school. I remember a conversation I had with my health teacher who was also the girls' basketball coach. In our discussion maybe he was trying to have a heart to heart, but he had a discussion with me that sat in my head strongly. He asked me what I was going to be when I grew up. I said a Professional Baseball player, with confidence. He proceeded to let me know about the millions of kids playing all over the world who were better than me, and how they eventually would be standing in way of achieving my dream. This conversation didn't have an immediate impact, but later became discouraging. Although, he was right, I didn't feel like it was the right time to have the conversation. Mr. Wolfe could have easily delivered the message but delivered it in a way that made me hopeful.

I don't believe Mr. Wolfe was aware of the power of his words; nor do I think teachers, in general, understand the power they possess. My experience with Wolfe taught me a lot on the power of words. When children hear adults talk, they are expecting leadership and guidance. That reputation is set immediately upon the first impression. Once respect is gained it is yours to be lost. Once respect is lost there is no way of it resurfacing. Children are the ultimate example of remembering how you made them feel. Children wear their emotions on their sleeves no matter the experience. Teachers must be conscious of their power and never lose the trust or respect of the student; nor should a teacher or mentor ever discourage a child from their dreams or capabilities. As a speaker, I must make the Teachers and faculty to be aware of this, but also, I must educate and empower the students on how to deal with these situations without giving up on themselves or giving in to the situation. These messages resonated with the children, because at some point— they felt it. The more I experience speaking, I learned that everyone is battling something in their lives, and not everyone knows how to combat whatever their situation is. People need ideas, inspiration, and studies. Good speakers provide the information and ideas needed that create the action.

When I was experiencing my darkest moments, it was oratory geniuses such as Les Brown and Zig Ziglar who gave me my hope and helped me identify my individual consciousness, and that in order to change, I had to change. Until then, I had no mentor or teacher feeding that knowledge into my psyche. Mr. Brown inspired me to dig deep into myself and rediscover what was missing. Dreams, aspirations, and a life of service using my gifts. Finding new avenues, new platforms, new networks, and new opportunities. To me this was power. No religion, no pity, no guilt, just pure hope. What Mr. Brown did for me was what I wanted to do for others. To this day, there is no better fulfillment. I want to awaken the dormant dreams of those who for whatever reason have given up on themselves. I want to show people that they can persevere through whatever scenario life has placed upon them and influence them to overcome. I truly believe that when we focus on ourselves, we begin to know truly who we are and what we are capable of. We can never run from our consciousness. The decisions we make create the lives we live and the experience we have daily. I plan to awaken millions to their own thought processes and how their history has patterns, and how knowledge inspires creativity.

It's amazing to me that Toastmasters has all-around taught me to get outside of my comfort zone. The only experience that I could relate it to would be standing naked in front of a crowd of people. The feeling of vulnerability can be a bit overwhelming but can be conquered. Through my Toastmasters experience, I have constantly put myself in uncomfortable experiences. Every contest I've performed in has been my weakness. My first was a humorous speech, and I am not at all a comedian, but I figured the experience would help me in my evolution of speaking. The first obstacle was finding something funny to talk about. The next was delivering a message through the humor. I was drawing blanks as of the creative mind was absent. I meditated on the thought and out of meditation came out the topic of meditation. Now, I needed to make it funny. I asked my wife and brother in law for ideas, and through brain- storming, we came up with three things that make people laugh and feel uncomfortable. One was farting, two was pooping, and three was falling. I choose pooping and now had to come up with a story of pooping and meditation, but I needed more humor. Then, I was on Facebook and a video I recorded and posted of my daughter looking and reaching under the bathroom door not giving her a break, popped on the screen, and that there was humor. Now, I had to put it all together in a story line, and honestly, to me, it was an award-winning speech with a great message regarding something I was passionate about. The speech went as follows:

DID YOU POOP TODAY?

I SAID DID YOU POOP TODAY?

GOOD! GOOD! GOOD!

You're supposed to poop daily.

Dr. Mariloma of a certain University says we should poop daily, some multiple times, some even more. A healthy digestive system can be life changing. It's a must to be aware of your health and after the age of 40 to get your prostate checked by your Doctor.

I love taking a DO DO. It's something about life taking control of my time and telling me I need to sit my butt down for a minute, or two, or three, or five, or until your legs get tingly and fall asleep. Many of us are having different activities and ways of distracting ourselves while we do the do. Some of us use this time to check the messages on our phone. First its text messages, then emails, then Facebook, Instagram, Snapchat, Twitter, Dracula, blah, blah, blah. Some read magazines, newspapers, articles, books, world star, TMZ, whatever flashes on your phone. Sometimes we are in a rush and forget to flush. With so many distractions, I would like to offer you my method— bear with me. First, allow me to thank God for privacy. Even in a public restroom, I have 4 walls narrowly around me. Now, look at this time as if the universe or God is demanding you take a time out. During this time make sure you are prepared. Never sit on the toilet without checking the amount of toilet paper. Next, make sure the door is locked. Next, make sure there is soap to wash your hands.

This next part is where things got controversial, but I thought it was hilarious and so did many in the audience. What I did was incorporate props. I had a chair there in front of the room, and under my slacks was a pair of shorts. I made sure they were my longest pair of basketball shorts and silver. During the speech, I pulled down my slacks and sat on the chair to mimic me taking a poop, but not exposing anything. They say you should always know your audience. This audience was predominantly white and over 50- years old, but when you're in a competition, you go with the material that has worked till that point.

I proceeded as I sat in the chair with my slacks at my ankles to increase the effectiveness of my visual. I said I love this time of privacy— I take this as a time to reflect and meditate. Ponder on the past, meditate on the moment, plan for the rest of the day, and prepare for what it may bring. Five minutes of meditation can calm the nerves, relieve anxiety, and help the mind create a plan. Meditation allows your mind to visualize and affirm action. (COURTESY FLUSH) Sometimes, you must deal with interruptions— if you have young children you've probably seen this before. (Picture of my daughter's fingers under the door. Then the view from the other side). I continued, by saying make this time all about you. Meditation is beneficial to your daily activities and decisions. As we go through the day, we allow shit to constantly build up in our minds. I ended the speech by saying sometimes we just need to let it out and flush it away.

Great speech, but not good enough to win, as I lost to a well-known Toastmaster in Las Vegas who told a story about superheroes having insurance with his down south twang accent. To me, his speech was good, but not better or funnier than mine. I got more laughs and delivered a message. In the end, I won second place, and my contest ended there. He went forward to the next round and competed at a higher level. Losing taught me a lesson— I still needed to get better and learn more, but also, I needed to control my anger. Although, I didn't show my anger, I was furious within. I felt feelings of jealousy and envy, and I needed to check myself before I said something to ruin my reputation. I sucked it up, smiled, congratulated the winner, and left before the event ended. As I drove home my wife and I discussed the competition. She believed I won as well. As we talked, we observed the experience in its totality. I wasn't supposed to win. My intention was to gather the experience, compete, step outside my comfort zone, and grow. With that experience, I definitely accomplished that. I proved to myself that I was able, and that no matter the result I delivered my message. My Toastmasters group was proud of me and they had more respect for me following the competition. With this confidence, all I could do was get better, and to having my wife's support increased the motivation. Life was definitely getting better, and as I was working diligently to become a better man, with that intention in mind I was learning and changing.

Not only was I changing, but so was Tiffany. After she accomplished the publishing of her book, her confidence was growing rapidly. Her grind became her book and her determination had her on every news station promoting her book signing and release. Her first book signing went amazing. We hosted it at a small used bookstore and before start time she had a line from the very rear of the store where she was located, all the way out of the door and past a couple of businesses. She had the hospital sponsorship and news coverage. She had become a big deal. Many people showing up from her Facebook page and purchasing books and taking pictures with her and Brazyl. I was very proud of her. She had a few other events locally as well, and the most memorable one was in Maryland. She attended The African American Author's Expo and was excited to get her book on the east coast. Our time there was great. When we are together working; we get shit done. I know how she thinks and pays attention to everything. When I'm with her I give her my best energy and support her proactively, causing her to up her game. She is a beast with her work ethic, so she always outperforms me when dealing in her element. The trip was fun and successful. I was super motivated and inspired for where we have been and where we were headed.

As we were both now chasing our dreams, and embracing the support from the community, life became a lot more hopeful. We would ride that wave for a while until the biggest bomb would drop on our marriage at a very devastating time of our life.

THE PAIN OF A MAN

7

THE BOMB AKA KARMA

"What happens in the dark always comes to light." Is a saying that my Egungun grandmother Inetter Sherow would say to me when I was a young boy. Before I didn't understand, but after my life experiences, I was forced to understand this logic. One morning in the beginning of September 2015, Tiffany received a message in her Instagram DM of a male profile appearing to be gay and claiming to be sleeping with me. The messages indicated that we were in a relationship and insinuated that I was gay and living this secret life. I had no idea who this was at first but somehow within the many messages, I was able to decipher who it really was and what they were really saying. I received messages as well. It was Lisa. The messages were telling me that I'd better tell Tiffany the truth before she exposes what happened. When I read the messages, I immediately felt an overwhelming sensation of heat. Everything within me was full of fear and decay. I was shocked, silent, and playing stupid at first. My mind was in full on panic mode. All I could do was think about what to say and how to say it. I was thinking of lies, thinking of the pain Tiffany would experience, thinking of what was going to happen with my family. This was the ultimate feeling of defeat, and this wasn't even the beginning. I could already feel the pain. Everything we built would be thrown away by a meaningless act. 9 years of marriage she thought I was loyal and faithful. Now, her worst fears of me cheating with my ex would be manifested.

No matter how much I wanted to lie, it was obvious that I had to tell the truth— before dropping this bomb, I decided it would be best to wait until the children were off to school. I left Tiffany in the garage to continue her investigation of the profile and the messages, while I went inside and got the kids ready for the day. While getting them ready it was a very emotional heartfelt moment, knowing that our days like this would possibly never be the same. Tiffany, still dumbfounded by what was going on, stayed home while I took the children to school. As I returned, she met me in the garage and the first thing I said to her was that I was going to be 100% honest with her and she would never be the same. I then told her to walk with me to the park. For some reason, I felt more comfortable in an open public setting. She agreed. As we walked, we were silent for a couple of minutes then I broke the silence by trying to make small talk. But she had no interest in hearing anything I was speaking about and remained silent. The entire time I was trying to build up the courage of telling the truth. That I had betrayed her and did exactly what she told me not to do, and with the person she told me I better not ever with.

Scenarios ran through my mind of how she would receive the information, how she would react. Would she be so angry as to make a scene, or breakdown and cry? The closer we walked to the park the more I slowed the pace, but Tiffany would speed it right back up. I could feel all my nerves activated as if they were preparing for pain. As we continued, we entered the park at an empty playground, as all the children were in school. We later sat at a park bench and without hesitation as I had rehearsed in my head on the way there. I said "Our life will never be the same after I tell you this but know that no matter what I've done in the past. I love you. But I did exactly what you told me not to do. That message you received is not from a male— I am not gay. That message is from Lisa and I need to tell you that I slept with her."

At that moment, you could hear her heart drop, her eyes began to water, and the tears began to fall. Then, the pain took over her body as she went limp, sinking into the bench. She said not a word and cried, cried hard, and I could feel it. All I could do was hold her and console her until she felt irritated by my touch and pulled away from me. Saying, "After all, we've been through together! After all the pain and sacrifice with our daughter! After three beautiful children! After almost 10 years of marriage!" The crying continued. This pain wasn't unfamiliar, nor was the cry. This was the similar pain I witnessed the night of the accident. She appeared to be broken, and that broke me. She would never have the same impression of me again. Up until that point, I was her superman, her protector, provider, and companion, and I could do no wrong. Now, with the mark of betrayal, what was once pure was no longer. Purification is divine— once it's contaminated; it is forever damaged, and I believe it takes a lifetime to repair, and I was willing to fight for my marriage. I had already began taking action, working on myself and making changes. I was no longer weak in certain areas that once ruled me. I was aware of myself and our relationship, and what areas that needed change and attention. I was no longer that person— I no longer had the mindset of a young boy.

No matter what I said she was hurt, and at that time it was best to be quiet. She wanted to know the story, but I decided not to share the details. Thinking this was the best approach to the pain she was already feeling. At some point she became annoyed with me and began to walk home, I caught up, but she needed some time alone. So, I fell back and followed from a distance not knowing the faith of our marriage. Not knowing if she would heal, and not knowing if I would ever be forgiven. All I did know is I was hurt, seeing the woman I loved back in pain, and because of me and my poor decisions. Decisions that ruin my family. Damn. I fucked up and these were my confessions.

The days that followed were interesting. She cried for nearly a week nonstop. Every time I would try and have small talk with her, she would break out in tears and leave the room. Then one day, the tears just stopped. I watched Tiffany do everything she could to keep her confidence up, but she was fighting within. Daily, she was taking her time to get dressed and put on makeup. Constantly taking selfie pictures and mirror photos and posting them on social media. It was obvious to me that she was seeking attention and approval or whatever was gratifying. Many times, she would get men flirting in her comment section or writing her in her DM. I would never say anything. How could I after what I had done? I was often complimenting her, but it was as if it didn't matter. I believe psychologically she didn't believe me. If I believed she was beautiful or attractive, then I wouldn't have looked elsewhere nor entertained someone else. What I once had was lost, but if she allowed me to win back her love, I would give my best effort.

A very interesting turn of events that occurred two weeks after, was when a childhood friend of Tiffany's was visiting for the weekend and needed somewhere to stay due to the weekend hotel rates being too expensive. We had a 2300 square foot home with an extra bedroom, so we had plenty of room— the timing was off but was perfect for Tiffany as it took her mind off the heartbreak she was feeling. The friendship they had together was different than most friendships. The other girl was young and full of life. She didn't have much responsibility and seemed to always be looking to have a good time. She was funny, outgoing, and adventurous. Just the personality Tiffany needed to be cheered up, because before then she would sleep in days and when she did wake up, she was disconnected and didn't do or say much to me or the kids. One thing I did notice about their interaction was how flirtatious they had become, and much of their conversation centered on sex. I'm not sure how things led up to the point where the conversation involved me, but out of nowhere, Tiffany had said that her friend wanted us. My first reaction was this a joke, but they clearly were not playing. I was completely surprised by this turn of events and opportunity, but I thought it was a test to see if I was attracted to the friend. My first reaction was rejection. Although, her friend was good looking and had sex appeal, I wanted to prove to Tiff that I was no longer on that, and willing to change— but this obviously wasn't about me and was something that she wanted. I remained hesitant and as the evening turned into the night it was clear that this was no test or joke.

After the kids went to bed we chilled in the backyard, which was our favorite place to hang out. The backyard was nicely decorated with patio furniture, tiki torches, and white Christmas lights to enhance the ambiance. We played music, had a few drinks, and the girls got even more flirty. Somehow one thing led to another and the girls were kissing. I sat back and watched for a while until I was told to join. At that point, any reservations or doubts I had regarding the situation were now gone. I was turned on and excited, and from that point, there was no turning back. Fully emerged in the situation I was for a short time, but then there was a moment that caused me to snap into consciousness. Although, I was told to join I followed Tiffany's lead and chose not to initiate anything. For fifteen to twenty minutes I was active and into the entire session, but I later got into my head, and what was supposed to be fun and satisfying, became a heavy burden on my conscious. The look and ambition on Tiffany's face was unlike I've ever seen. There was no doubt that she was enjoying herself and as for me I just fell back and watched as if I was turned on just by the opportunity to watch them, but as I looked on I felt some type of way. I was watching a complete change and manifestation of another person. My betrayal had hurt Tiffany so bad that now she was plotting and patient. This woman knew everything about me. All my flaws, secrets, weaknesses, and habits. She knew she was the object of my desires and knew how to use sex to control me— but what she wasn't aware of, was my immediate desire to change and becoming aware of those actions and feelings. My mind became strong and aware of all energy of the moment. Well, all the energy that I could feel. My empathy had grown to understand the emotional experience of all involved in a situation, and I was aware enough of when it was necessary for me to take the L and suffer so that she or anyone else didn't have to. During this time, I became very good at suffering.

This new mental mindset brought awareness, and I deserved the pain.

One question I always asked myself was to what extent shall I allow myself to punish myself? I really got to the point where I began to take many L's, but what I had chosen to do was dedicate myself to getting our relationship back in order, and proving to her that I loved her, and was in the process of change. I was already making changes to fix my thoughts of what caused these things to happen, so she wouldn't ever have to worry about it again, but who was I kidding. She was hurt and trust she had no more. I paid attention to her every move. I began to spend more time working from home. The job at that time gave me that type of flexibility. In the beginning, I gave her space, but made it a point to acknowledge her and tell her that I loved her and was very regretful of my decisions. I wanted her to realize that I was more aware of the consequences of my decisions and wouldn't jeopardize us again. I also understood how important it was for me to not allow her to lose her self-confidence, and not feel as if she was in competition with anyone else. I also wanted to know if she forgave me, or even if she could forgive me. Seeing her hurting daily was hurting me, and I was willing to put in all the effort necessary if she was willing to foresee a positive future together. We needed to have this discussion. There was no need for us wasting time together if we were not heading in the right direction, and if there was some hope, I was willing to give my all. Although it was only a short time ago since she found out about what happened, and I broke her heart. I made the mistake of having the discussion too soon. I laid it all on the table past, present, and future. I painted the picture of the timeline, from the beginning of us coming together and being so in love, to the point of bitterness, and resentment.

We discussed our sacrifices and all that we had been through. We discussed our family and what we created. We discussed our perseverance up to this moment and what it would be like to finally quit. We discussed everything, putting every thought, issue, and concern in the open, and in the end, she said that she forgave me, but needed time to heal. Quoting me saying "Things will never be the same." Like I said earlier, if there was hope, I was willing to put in the effort. One thing for sure, I didn't want to experience was us separating again. We once separated back in 2007-2008. This was a very difficult time for us, but it was necessary. Very young, we were full of ego and had no respect for one another. This was like a one-year break that resulted in us both learning much about ourselves, but realizing we were meant to be together. During that break, I lost so much of myself. First, I lost my motivation, then my career as a police officer. After that, I lost my identity. Going through that experience was humbling. The freedom that came with that life needed to be approached with maturity. I was just trying to satisfy my cravings and heal my pain in any way I could without going against my beliefs. Single life is fun, but not for me, due to there being too many options and opportunities, on top of that I seem to attract the single women who are searching for commitment and fall for me quickly.

After a month passed, my birthday was arriving, and things seemed to be getting better. The family was still together, and Tiffany was beginning to come around. As I was indecisive of what I wanted to do, she had known I became very spiritual and was studying, meditating, and practicing my beliefs. As genius as Tiffany is, she still had questions and needed understanding and answers. So as my birthday arrived, she said not to make plans at 1 pm, as she had a surprise and would be taking me somewhere special. Anxiously, I go through the morning staying busy so that the time goes faster. At 1230 we left home with the kids secured with a babysitter. As I sit on the passenger side while Tiffany drives, I do my best to get her to tell me where we were going, and she wouldn't give me a clue. I then became annoying like a young kid playing the guessing game, and never got the right answer. The drive was about 15 minutes from home, and we arrived at a psychic shop. Not being completely in the moment I got out the car hyped. This was our second time visiting a shop together as I had taken her to a psychic at the very beginning of us dating. I've always been intrigued by psychics and their spiritual gifts and wisdom. I am a true believer in their power and existence, but none publicly. There are some special people that you can only find through word of mouth and amongst certain tribes that exist according to their niche. People who can hear things that others cannot. Can interpret mystical things that others cannot. Then, there are those who can tell the future. At that moment we were on a mission to discover something. When we walked in the sign on the door said CC'S. We were greeted by her assistant, a mixed African American girl with long hair in a bun, and a busty chest. She made the place feel tranquil and then offered us tea.

As we sat in the waiting area the assistant asked if one or both would be getting a reading. The plan was just me, but after talking to the assistant she very much insisted that Tiffany get one as well. Tiffany was on the fence about it for the most part, and then CC called me back to receive my reading. As I walked in the door, she has this shocked look on her face as is I had the aura of Jesus around me. I stopped, and she says, "You are not even here for you, your Angel's brought you here and would like to meet you." Speechless, I take in the information and try to process it, and eventually in my mind,

I became curious. A voice inside me said speak, but another said just listen and see where this goes. She says you've been doing a lot of spiritual work, and most people who come into her shop have an identity crisis and want to figure who they are. Me on the other hand, I knew who I was, but I needed to get to know the energy that has been supporting me. She tells me their secret names and physical attributes. She advises me of the ways they have supported me, and after every scenario, I could align a time that something similar had occurred. She seemed very legit and I was in awe with her gift. As she read me more, she started asking a few questions and got into my trauma. She knew I had a kid that was hurt in a car accident but wasn't aware of the details. She just knew that survival was because of the work of a female angel. After the emotional stuff, we got into love life. With love life, I was open and willing to be 100% honest. She saw me happy, but not fulfilled. That's when I began to complain about my wife and the things she did not do, or I was not happy with. She then said she saw infidelity in the past, but nothing as of recent. I said nothing and I guess my hard pause was enough to make her understand that I wasn't comfortable with the conversation.

We moved forward and she asked if I loved my wife. I told her, yes, but I was unhappy with who my wife had become after the accident. She said she understood, but when she saw Tiffany, she could feel her pain. She said on the inside she is broken, hurt, and depressed. I then opened up and told her about my infidelity with Lisa and described the incident of Tiffany finding out. I discussed my regrets and resentments as if this lady was a magic genie. She said many things giving advice and telling my fortune. The one thing she said to me that stood out the most was when she said I should get to know Jesus. This made no sense to me, because what I learned up to this point was that Christians viewed psychics as mediums for witchcraft. So why would she be telling me to get to know him? As a young child, I grew up in the church. Grandma had me at St. Paul AME two or three times a week. I spent many years in the children's ministry. My grandmother was in the choir and my grandfather in law Melvin was a Deacon. I was too young to remember my beliefs at the time, but chances were that I was willing to do whatever made Grandma proud and happy. As I got older, I touched on religion here and there. Enough to make myself familiar and enough to understand, but not enough to make a commitment. I always knew that when I needed hope I could go to church, but when CC said this to me, it made me curious to figure out the reason. As we closed out my session, she invited Tiffany in the room. The first thing she says to her is how she could see the hurt of her heart beaming from her aura. She asks what it was that was bothering Tiffany, and Tiffany had told her about having her heart crushed, feelings of betrayal, loss of trust, and inability to think positively of our future. CC asked if I was willing to be honest while she was present and asked a few questions. I agreed not knowing where this was headed. I just knew that before things got better, they had to get worse, and after hearing my success reading, whatever happened up to this point we would get through. CC then asked with Tiffany present the following questions. "Do you love Tiffany?" I immediately said Yes. She continued her questions. "Do you believe Tiffany is your soulmate?" Yes. "Are you still conducting in that behavior? No. Do you still talk to the woman? No. "Have you had infidelities in the past?" No. Is she the only one? Yes.

"You and I both know that's not true Mr. Ward. Are you sure there wasn't anyone else?" CC says. I pause… Super nervous I start to recognize my body tension and heart rate begin to increase. Then, I admit to an affair I had with a former coworker, where I managed security at this call center, but that had ended long ago, and I was no longer in contact. CC then said who else? I said no one. CC then had her damn nerve to tell me I was lying. I looked at her with a look on my face like MF if you don't shut the hell up and chill with this interrogation. This is not the First 48. Whatever I had done, I wasn't doing anymore, and had no interest in doing so again. Tiffany stayed silent with tears falling from her face. She then sent me to this crystal bed to lay on for healing, but I didn't feel anything, but anger within. Tiffany stayed in the room to have her one on one session. 45 minutes to an hour later we were done. When Tiffany met me in the lobby, I looked at the reaction on her face to gauge her level of hurt, but she had no pain. The look on her face was strength from recovery, and determination to move forward. When we got into the car we were not as open as usual. You could feel the tension and

I felt embarrassed and resentful. Somehow, we started with small talk, then Tiffany says to me, "You're not going to like what she said

Regarding our future. She said we were going to break up, date other people, but live in the same house."

"Hell no!" I said. "For what? I've changed. Those aren't my issues anymore."

Tiffany says, "I'm just telling you what she said."

The rest of the ride home was silent as we listened to the radio. I was in denial. This birthday gift turned out to be horrible. Although, she is psychic, in the end, we have the last decision. I was even more eager now to prove my love, but I was not willing to sacrifice the love I had for myself. I wanted to be better, stronger, and live within my passion. I guess it was time to see where this spirit thing would take me.

8

SAVE ME

As I was making changes, I was very adamant about learning as I was making the adjustments in this area of my life. One network that influenced my spirituality was Oprah's OWN network. She weekly had a new guest on her show called Super Soul Sunday. Each guest much different than the other discussing their own story and spiritual experience. Most are authors who are part of Oprah's Book Club. I love this show because you can tell that Oprah is a fan of each guest. When interacting with the guest, she is prepared and listens to their experiences and perspectives in a non-judgmental way. This allows the viewer to gain insight into their philosophy and learn that we are all in a different experience with a common goal and lifestyle, in search of a connection with the Divine. I enjoy the lessons taught and the inspiration to change, accept, and love. Many of the guests I have purchased their books and read them gaining a little more philosophy to utilize in my day to day decisions and actions. My favorites have been lessons taught by the Greats Maya Angelou and Wayne Dyer; may they rest in peace. Eckhart Tolle, Don Miguel Ruiz, Gary Zukav, amongst others. I loved the concept of spirituality and is being the God source within. This helped me in my spirituality and understanding. Nothing too tough, just change my character and be conscious of my conscience.

Things changed though after Tiffany's book "From Tragedy to Testimony," was released and Pastor Dr. Robert Fowler Sr. of Victory Missionary Baptist offered to buy a large order of 200 books, we just needed to give our testimony to all three Sunday services and partake in a book signing after church concluded. We agreed, this was a perfect opportunity to tell our story in front of a powerful congregation and make some much-needed money. The Pastor's support was very successful as Tiffany sold the majority of the books we had in the stock. During this time, spiritually I was looking for more and was tired of being alone on my journey. After hearing a sermon by Pastor Fowler, I was inspired to return to future services for the next few weeks, and sermon after the sermon was straight fire. Each one speaking directly to my spirit. He touched on Moses splitting the Red Sea and the Pharaohs. He spoke on Jesus and his disciples, and the craziest story in the Bible where God makes a deal with Satan, and allows Satan to destroy a Faithful Servant's life, but he can't hurt him, in order to prove a point and show the ultimate definition of faith. Hearing these stories gave a feeling of hope and inspiration. If a man could lose everything he loves and becomes happy because he receives multiple of what he had before after suffering due to a deal with Satan and his loyalty. Then, maybe my life and all the crap I had experienced wasn't so bad after all. Maybe God was testing my faith and calling me to him through this tragedy and being there with this monetary opportunity to receive a blessing at a time in need. Honestly, it was a blessing, and answered prayers, but with everything comes something, and dealing with spirit, you can be in for a ride of your life.

The more I went to church the more I wanted to become a part of the congregation. Plus, I had noticed a high level of hierarchy that was easily accessible there. Many of the community leaders were members of Victory. Victory to me is the best church in the Las Vegas Valley. Just my opinion, plus I haven't attended every church in the valley. I have heard many preachers preach through 88.1 FM on Sundays, and Pastor Fowler to me is the best. Maybe it's because he connects with my spirit and his style is not superficial. Not to mention their band and choir are anointed on another level. Their play alone awakens the spirit, then Pastor Fowler comes with an amazing message. After one sermon, I decided to rejoin the church and take another try at the Christian faith. I was becoming a better man and needed more philosophy and structure. At Victory when people are ready to join the church, they usually wait for the time Pastor calls those who are in need of prayer or would like to dedicate their lives to Christ and join the church. This came with some encouragement from the choir singing a welcoming melody, as a preacher would say encouraging and inspiring words. Such as "Jesus hears your pain, and he knows your suffering. As he suffered before dying on the cross— let him take away your pain, would you come forward? No one is judging you; this is about your relationship with him, and all you have to do is walk forward." At times of pain and turmoil, this moment is heavy on the conscious, especially if you're deep in your emotions, and you need some hope. The church is a great place for healing. To have an entire congregation supporting you and praying for you. Knowing that intention alone is enough to make a person feel better. If the mind has a pain of conscious guilt taking the problem to Jesus and asking for forgiveness. Knowing that he forgives, a person can be relieved of that inner guilt of the possibility of being punished or going to hell in the afterlife. This philosophy alone I believe is what prevents people from committing suicide, which makes sense in the world we live in, because our minds are constantly enticed and seduced in following everything opposite of what is in the Bible. Then, when we mess up and try to get right, we go to church and learn how we have been spiritually and culturally bamboozled. Learn some discipline, gather some understanding, breakdown, and renew the mind with a new philosophy.

My Christian experience was empowering. Yes, Buddhism, Hinduism, and Enlightenment had their healing potential and a certain level of appreciation to the universe that to me seemed very basic but gave me knowledge of self and consciousness. Once I achieved that, I needed more philosophy, and with my new love and increased ability to read, I was ready to take on the Bible— I had never really read the Bible, but had the same one for over 10-years, which was given to me by a client of mine when I was working pest control in California. She was an older African American woman who lived alone, and every month when I would service her home, she would offer some form of encouragement. I value these people in life because these are the ones you never forget. The day she gave me my Bible was prior to me quitting my job there and moving to Las Vegas to become a police officer. I found the Bible tucked away in the garage storage area, dusty, but leather on the cover so no damage. Honestly, it was in such good condition you could tell that I never read the thing, but this walk would be different. I decided to submerge myself into the book and get out of it as much as I could. The Bible I have is an (NIV) and at the bottom has many translations on words and sentences just in case the reader isn't fully inclined to be able to comprehend the text. I admit in the beginning it was rough. I was constantly using the key at the bottom, which didn't bother me, because I was really trying to gain understanding and study the text. I started from the very beginning. The first page was signed TO: BRANDON WARD, FROM MRS. WATERS. She wrote in an old school fancy cursive in blue ink. I'll forever remember her kind heart and gesture.

I began reading 30- minutes at a time, and the longer I went through the process the more my reading duration increased. I remember I would sit in the garage and read for hours or stop by the park and read for another hour. I had made it my goal to read the entire Bible from front to back within a year. This was a huge task because the book was challenging, intimidating, and huge. I started from the very beginning and at first, I was confused, but eventually got the hang of the verbiage. This was similar to my police academy experience were I at first had a difficult time comprehending the terminology, but eventually, my mind got the hang of it. With the Bible, I was reading through it rapidly, but also, I was becoming very involved with the church. I was attending Sunday service, followed by a Tuesday Bible study weekly. The more I learned, the more I felt myself transforming. I was changing and becoming a better man. I was trying to uplift myself, but also my intention was to prove to Tiffany that I really had changed, and would never hurt again, but this approach completely backfired. Tiffany was never really into church and religion. She was about love and loyalty, and I had betrayed her. With Christianity when you have faith, the psychology with worshiping Jesus is to confess to him your sins and ask for forgiveness, and it shall be granted. Great for the psychology of the sinner, but when that sin involves hurting another, forgiveness doesn't come that easy. I was empowered mentally as my self-guilt had diminished spiritually, but Tiffany was battling with forgiveness. It seemed like the happier and healthier I became, the more she despised me. She couldn't stand to see me happy— the look on her face was of disgust, while I was feeling amazing.

The church at that time was a big deal for me, I had plans to move up the ranks of the congregation. Tiffany on the other hand could care less. Many times, the pastor would be speaking a great sermon with a great message. But because Tiffany had to take anxiety medication just to take the ride in the car, I would look over and she would be knocked out as if she were sitting on the couch. I would complain which would start an argument, then she would reprimand me by not going the next Sunday. We went from going as a family, to many times just me and the kids. After all the discussions, after all the fights, and after all the encouragement, she wouldn't budge. After a few occasions, it was apparent to me that my wife had checked out. She wasn't interested in anything I was learning or experiencing, nor was she interested in my growth. Every now and again she would participate, but I swear it was like pulling teeth. She would wake up late and only focus on herself while I would get everyone ready including myself, then feed them so they wouldn't complain or have me buying fast food. Her lack of help would have me so frustrated. But what do I look like starting an argument before church? If I did, she would use it as an excuse not to go. I desperately needed her help, and we desperately needed to hear the word. We were falling apart. Growing distant each day because each day I was growing and becoming better. I was better, but I was bitter as well. I felt like I was constantly skating on thin ice, and there was something about Christianity that made me feel a level of hate for those who were non-believers or didn't follow. I felt like they were vessels of Satan. Here to distract me from becoming my highest self and impede the path of my journey.

I see where this can be destructive to many marriages and relationships all over the world. You never hear people discuss this publicly, but when people of different beliefs become one, at some point this can disrupt the marriage. When things are going well you couldn't distinguish, but when tragedy strikes or it's time to perform the ritual, faith brings philosophy.

Philosophy brings guidelines and impactful living. If the two individuals are not what the Bible calls "Equally yoked," then this causes many problems. It is like playing the same game with a different rule book. Battling with this alone was a psychological war. There were so many days where I felt like my wife was an enemy. The more she was giving up, the more I started giving into my thoughts. I was getting in tune with myself spiritually. Every feeling and emotion that I could identify with, I researched it. I found that every emotion or condition had been experienced and researched at some point, and someone published their findings in books. I started reading books by Robert Greene on psychology. Learning my patterned and the patterns of others, and how they manipulate through life based on what has worked for them in the past. I began to be able to read people's actions, identifying strengths and weaknesses. I focused on what distracted me and others, and what caused them to lose focus or break down. Learning the strength of a person's crutch and how reliant they are upon certain things in order to function or operate at a higher level. Everything that I was experiencing, and learning was giving me a clear understanding. The more I learned the more I understood, which brings me to a thought I had come across while I read about King Solomon in the Bible. He was a wise and handsome king, loved by the people, and had very few enemies. His character was the one character I admired most throughout the Bible. I wanted to be exactly like him. I remember praying to God to have Wisdom like Solomon. Far-fetched for non-collegiate graduate, but with faith anything is possible. The level of determination I received after that prayer was proof of the power of prayer, because since that day I have continuously learned something new every day, either reading or lectures.

Another issue that faith helped me to deal with was my anger. Although, I remained positive, my level of anger was to the max. Life was kicking me in the gut and going to church made me realize how fed up I really was. According to the good book I was doing everything wrong. This thought humbled me as it made me feel like I wasn't good enough. I had to get rid of who I thought I was in order to become who I wanted to be. I was a ratchet man. As my mind began to believe this, I slowly began to crumble. My ego was gone, and the only fight I had left in me was a conviction in religion, which later led to a curiosity of knowledge and psychology. The more I studied the more my mind shifted and expanded and adding meditation to the process gave me the ability to identify the emotional shift as well.

Although, I was changing it seemed the better I became. But the more progress I made; the more upset Tiffany would get. At church, we were already members, but the kids had not yet been baptized. The more I studied the more I wanted the kids to have that protection. The way I have seen it was that to baptize them would release them from facing transgressions for my sins, by accepting Jesus's sacrifice. After discussions with Tiffany, we decided we would get the kids baptized after school ended for summer in June 2016. This was a very interesting time leading to that day, because home life was becoming weird— it was obvious that we were growing apart. I was becoming more and more of a devout Christian and was walking with Christ and Tiffany was becoming more distant. The more I followed the philosophy of Christianity, the better I felt within my conscience. For the past year, I had been suffering from the guilt of the pain I caused and witnessing my wife fall out of love with me. To have someone who once worshipped you, no longer give a damn about you, is an eye-opening humbling experience. Especially when you seek that love and attention, and you become accustomed to it. Not only that, but my mother and my relationship have been rocky as well, mainly because of my relationship with Tiffany, but to be honest I have "Mommy Issues." Similar to "Daddy Issues," but mine stems from a place of love, trust, and manipulation. Now, that I mentioned this, and my mind is breaking it down I have to discuss this in a later chapter.

But let's get back to the philosophy of the love of Jesus, because when in that mind space you can overcome any pain within as you come to expect it, the only problem is that the forgiveness of the person you hurt is based on their own trust and belief system, and the way my wife had been acting her intentions were for me to suffer.

Things were constantly changing, and I was taking notice of all her actions. She was into all the weird shit. All the fake reality TV shows, constantly on social media, neglecting home again, and getting mad when I said something to her, always texting, and no intimate connection to sex. Just going through the motions. But when she would get ready for work, she would take two hours and get super dolled up. All for her phone sales job sitting in a cubicle. Red flag! Plus, if her mind thinks it, she somehow must express it, and she was giving me the signs. Although, often in code, she was letting it out. I would ask her about her day, and she would proceed to tell me about the new people that were recently hired in the department above hers in upgrades. She said they must have gone to some modeling agency to recruit the new employees, because the new staff looked like supermodels. She had taken an interest in this new female employee who was also a personal trainer. She then showed me the girls Instagram photos in which she was stunningly beautiful. I took a mental note and proceeded to watch her carefully. After a couple of weeks, she was still taking the extra effort of getting ready, but now she was becoming more distant, and had taken interest in promotion into upgrades, which was more money, but different hours. I also noticed that after a couple of weeks she stopped calling me on her lunch break and began texting. I had an issue with that, because before she would call and talk to me the entire break. When she wouldn't call me, I would call her, and she would rush me off the phone. Something was definitely up, and she was changing more and more by the day creating distance. When she was home her head remained looking down, she was constantly on her phone, and when I would complain about it, she'd say she was working. My question was working on what? There were no results, no new social media post, and no engagement, nothing that indicated work. This made me even more suspicious. It was obvious to me that she was lying. As I questioned her, even more, she became more uncomfortable. This caused her to become more defensive and started saying stuff like she is grown and could do whatever she wanted. This made me even more upset but being that I was into the Word of God I was able to control my temper and remain patient. I had come to the point where my prayers became, "God whatever is happening in the dark, please allow it to come to light." You must be careful what you pray for because God will definitely show up and expose what's in the dark.

In the summer of 2016, my walk with Christ was strong. I had just finished reading the entire Bible front to back and had a clear understanding of the context. One thing I strongly believed in, was getting the children baptized. I wanted to release them from my sins and wrongdoings. I always had it on my conscience that Brazyl getting hit was God's punishment to me. Although, she suffered physically. I was suffering entirely— I felt like my whole world had been ransacked and turned upside down, and I no longer wanted my family to suffer. So, in June, I scheduled for Reverend Jordan of Victory Missionary Baptist Church to baptize my babies. As a Christian father, this was a beautiful experience. Seeing the children in all white, dancing to the gospel music, and having a congregation supporting us was empowering. For me, it was a very spiritual experience. Each child one by one lined up behind the pool pit awaiting their turn to be dunked in a small pool of water the size of a large Jacuzzi. Even if they didn't understand what was going on, I wanted them to partake in the RITUAL. Once each child was finished, I could feel the relief subconsciously. This call for celebration and I was excited. I just knew things were getting better and would eventually fall in alignment. Boy was I wrong!

The arguments arrived the following Monday. The bitterness was apparent and after a few days of fighting and disagreements. By Wednesday Tiffany was saying she needed a break. I thought this was just her blowing smoke, but by Thursday she had arranged to leave home and to stay at her friend Karen's house for a week. I disagreed with her decision, but by doing so it was like pulling teeth. She had already made up her mind and determined to leave. Something within me said not to fight it. If she needed a break, allow her to take that break to save our marriage. By Friday, her shit was packed for the week and she was gone. The hardest thing was explaining to the kids that Mommy was leaving temporarily. They wanted to understand, and all I could say was that Mommy was unhappy and would be back. Alone with the kids for the weekend I was devastated. Tiffany wasn't answering my calls or text messages. I then became curious and was driving past Karen's house at night when the kids were asleep to see if she had any visitors or if I could catch anything. No one was there, but heavy on my conscience I had to do more digging. That's when I decided to check the phone records, and what I discovered would become my worst nightmare and the biggest shock ever.

I literally had to make myself hate her in order to relieve my pain. In the past, I would just do something conniving in private, but living according to Christian philosophy I had to deal with it and think this too shall pass, but it wasn't. Things continued to get worse, and eventually, she checked out.

9

LOST ON THE RIGHT PATH

S itting at the computer, my jaw dropped, and suspicion had risen. There was one number that Tiffany was in constant contact with via text message. I then checked the call log and the number appeared multiple times for long durations with a few short ones. It was always an outgoing call. As I checked the times it was usually when I would leave home according to schedule. During this time, I was very active. Often going to work on speaking, church, Bible study, health, or work. Being that my life was on a schedule she would call this number as soon as I would leave. The number was unfamiliar, and my curiosity caused me to want to call the number and see who would answer. Before calling though I needed to think this through. What if I hear a man's voice on the other end? How should I react? What if it was a women's voice on the other end? How should I question it? A voice came into my head that said to log into Tiffany's Gmail account from my phone and choose to upload the contacts and BOOM her entire contact list by name popped up. I then typed in the number on the phone and the number was saved under a female name from an organization we did events with. Loren. Puzzled I decided to call the number, and on the other end picked up a male. I asked, "Can I speak to Loren?" His deep voice replied, "You have the wrong number." I hung up. WTF! I let it set in for a minute as my anger elevated even more within. I tried to calm down, but I got angrier. I needed answers. I then called Tiffany and asked her for the number to the organization lady to inquire about an upcoming event. She paused, then proceeded to give me a different number and asked why. Clearly learning that something was up.

I sat on the feeling for as long as I could trying to avoid confrontation, but the irritation was too excessive. I had to call the original number back and get some answers, so I called the guy, and he answered on the first ring. Before getting all emotional and blowing up, I remained calm and told the dude who I was, and that I was Tiffany's husband. He said, "I heard a lot about you, and your wife and I have become friends." He said he had a girlfriend and he was going through something with her, so they had something to relate to, but he wouldn't tell me where they met. As he was on the phone I drove to Karen's house where Tiffany was and had him on speaker. I knocked on the door and Karen answered. I told her to have Tiffany come outside, because I didn't want to create a scene on the inside. With the guy on the speakerphone, Tiffany was shocked. I demanded answers, and while doing so my anger level was to the max. He remained calm and said, "This is you guy's issue," and said calmly on the phone to Tiffany if she needed him later to give him a call. He then ended the call and it was just me and Tiffany outside. Looking at her in her face she had an "I don't give a fuck" smirk. I paid attention to my inner dialogue, and honestly, Although I have never been violent toward her, I was thinking about knocking her muthafucking head off her shoulders. She gave me some lame excuse, and while she was talking, I noticed she was still wearing her wedding ring. I don't know how I did it, but while upset I precisely grabbed the ring off her finger, and along with mine threw them both as far as I could. So far that it was pointless to ever look for them again. I had thoughts of murder on mind, so I got into my car and drove back home before I did something that would destroy my life forever. As I left, she was upset and crying, but I didn't care. I just needed to get back home with my three kids.

That ride home was brutal. I had never felt this pain in my life. I felt betrayed, played, and couldn't stop crying. I just wanted to be reckless. When I got home, I grabbed my baseball bat and beat everything that was in the backyard. I took the canvas, framed wedding pictures, anything within grasp that had her face on it I destroyed it. The loud bangs and sounds awoke the neighbors, and when I saw their lights come on, I went into the garage stuck in my mind and my thoughts. I was too embarrassed to talk to anyone, so I just prayed to God, and as I did so, I felt the anger subside.

There is something about the energy of prayer that can transform a moment quickly. It's as if the mind immediately searches for a place of peace and healing. My heart rate was accelerated, I was breathing extremely heavy, and my world felt as if it was closing in. I had never in my life felt so many emotions at once, but what was worse was that I had no one to help me. No one to talk to, no one telling me it would be okay, except for a little voice in my head. The pain was unbearable, so I called the weed man, and 30 minutes later, I was as high as a kite. Unable to move I just sat there and meditated on the feeling. My mind began to operate the emotions, which allowed me to focus on each one individually, instead of everything pouring in all at once and becoming overwhelmed. As I meditated, I was no longer focusing on the problems, but the solutions, and first I had to deal with acceptance. Resistance was too heavy of a burden on the mind. The "why me" approach was not going to work here. My mind immediately located the thought that this was what I deserved. No matter how much I changed, the pain that I inflicted on my wife was bound to resurface and come back to haunt me. My Christian religious mind didn't understand. I had changed everything about myself, and asked Jesus for forgiveness, and the way things were going I had no inner guilt. It had been eight to nine months since Tiffany found out about my infidelities, which had occurred fifteen months prior to her finding out. Although, I had put myself through the process of transformation, it wasn't enough for what she was feeling.

Prior to Tiffany leaving, although life outside of the home was going great and I was discovering my gifts and purpose. Home life was miserable, I could tell that she was battling something within. She paid me no attention and when I would be in her presence. My empathy could feel the hurt and disgust within. Seeing the person you love hurting, because of the pain you caused is damaging to your soul. No matter how hard I tried, or how much I prayed, she wore the pain on her face like make up foundation— to have the person who once adored everything about you, now dispose of you is a feeling like no other. Although, she went through the motions and showed support where she chose to, I could feel her not being present. She wasn't proud of my accomplishments, wasn't supportive of my aspirations, and despised my times of happiness. My approach to life was one day at a time and to find joy when and wherever I could. This took spiritual warfare daily. From the time I woke up, I immediately prayed, followed by my meeting with the mirror, telling myself I love you, followed by my I AM (Affirmation) statements. I would then take my vitamins, put on ambient music, and meditate. After meditation, I would read The Bible or some type of self-help spirituality book by T.D. Jakes, Joyce Mayer, Wayne Dyer, Eckhart Tolle, or the white guy who preached on TV. Following that, I would work out or take my dog for a walk. All before the family woke up in the morning. This became my daily ritual, which would prepare my mind for the remainder of the day. This type of inspiration made acceptance easier, but still, I loved my wife and had made all these changes so she would know I would never hurt or betray her again—but in the end, the human psychology would win.

Tiffany had met someone new that fit the physical make up of what she desired. Tall, dark, handsome, with a beard, which was the popular look at the time. They both had something in common, which I was told that his girlfriend of many years had supposedly cheated in him in the past. That commonality gave them something to relate to, which brought up old feelings of betrayal and pain, which caused her emotions to arise like trauma or PTSD. I know this feeling all too well, because when I had my infidelities I never lied and said I was single. I would honestly confide in someone about my issues with my relationship, and they would offer support and encouragement. The person would say something like you don't deserve that, or you deserve better, which would subconsciously have you thinking that there is a much better life that exists outside of the relationship or marriage. I was constantly thinking the grass must be greener on the other side, and I'm sure Tiffany had reached that point as well. Acceptance was beneficial but would become more and more difficult by the day.

What hurt me the most was witnessing how the separation was affecting my children. For a father who was active in their life daily, those days they were away crushed me. Being in that big ass house alone with my dog, made me feel extremely lonely. I felt like Will Smith in the movie "I am Legend." I was so used to hearing the kids playing, fighting, yelling, and always needing Daddy to fix a problem. I began to hate silence and kept all the TV'S on in the house. I also had this huge king size bed that now was just me. No wife to hold on to or rub on, and no sex. As a Scorpio with a highly sexual appetite, this was extremely difficult. Sex was my way of overcoming depression at times, and now that I was a devout Christian, and my wife was gone, I had to discover new ways of overcoming this feeling. No porn, no random sexual encounters, no masturbation.

I honestly began to play myself. For some reason, Tiffany told me Karen didn't want the kids at her house due to her working the grave shift at her job. So as a father I choose to have Tiffany come to the house to watch the kids on her days and she slept on the couch. This was a gift and a curse because she would be on the couch on her phone all night texting away. Then when she fell asleep, she would put her phone inside the pillowcase she was sleeping on. I would find every reason to go downstairs just so that I could see her. I wanted to talk to her, touch her, hold her, and feel her body next to mine, but it was as if I didn't even exist.

She never budged. No sex, no kissing, nothing, and this felt like torture. This would go on for three days, then on the afternoon of the fourth day, she would be back at Karen's house doing her thing. I would have the kids the rest of the week to myself. During my days, we would never even hear from Tiffany. I became very stalkerish, constantly checking her social media profile to see what she was doing and who she was talking to. During this time, she pretty much laid low from Facebook. Facebook was weird, because we had received a nice sized following of people who admired our family, after all, we had been through. Our entire identity revolved around our family and our perseverance. Tiffany's book "From Tragedy to Testimony" was all about that. How we made it through the storm and remained stronger through this process. The cover of the book was a photo of our family, and now that had all stopped. She was no longer selling, nor even promoting the book.

Where she was active was where I wasn't active. She was into Instagram and Snapchat. I desperately attempted to hack her Facebook, but she had changed her password, and the only way for me to get the information, she had to get an email and generate a code that sent you a text message. Facebook's reset policy is very thorough and strict. What I was able to do though was hack her Instagram. By doing so, I had access to her entire account and was able to access her messages and the majority of her activity. By being able to monitor the things she commented on, and the things she liked. I was able to track her interest, and although she was saying she was just taking a break, everyone knew she was now available. Men were constantly in her DM "shooting their shot," I didn't expect anything less. She was beautiful and definitely feeling herself. She built herself esteem back up as she was taking much better care of herself. She was healthy and had sexy ass curves. She wore her hair in blond highlighted locks that were long and gave her an exotic look with her green eyes. Her makeup stayed on point as she was wearing that expensive Mac brand that you see women getting applied at the mall. Her nails stayed done, as she still had her gel nail set with the blue light machine. She then had access to a whole new wardrobe now that she was over Karen's house, and many of the outfits complimented her body perfectly. Tiffany was constantly taking selfies, and if her body was a business, she was marketing herself well. She was super attractive and had crazy sex appeal. It was crazy to see how many men and women were waiting for the opportunity, and she was soaking it all in.

By studying her Instagram movements, I was able to discover who she had her eyes on. There was this tall, dark, and handsome guy, whose profile was private. He played basketball, was religious according to the content he would post, and had a Filipino girlfriend which he had been dating for years according to their photos on his and her profile. Tiffany was constantly liking his post, but never leaving a comment, and she never liked any of the post that featured both of them. I figured this was the guy she was talking to on the phone for hours. I wasn't active on Snapchat, but where I wasn't, she was. When her days with the children would arrive, she would come back to the house. I did as much as I could to stay away in the daytime. But in the evening, I would come home, and she would act as if I weren't even there. The only time we would cross paths was when I would be in the garage working out or doing my thing, then she would come out to the garage for her smoke break. I would attempt to use this time to talk to her, to apologize, and try to get her to come back home, but she wasn't having it. Her wall was up. Nothing I said positive would be received, but once frustration would kick in, I would say something that she disapproved of and she would run with that energy. It didn't matter how much I said I loved her, or said I was sorry. The more I tried the further the distance she would create. She would be on Snap Chat taking pictures, I would place myself in the background, and she would immediately delete that post. This told me that whoever she was communicating with was on there, and she didn't want me to be seen. This would make me so sad that the pain would turn into anger. I would say something while feeling that energy, and she would use those words as another layer of the wall she had put up. This was driving me crazy. She did give me hope at times by coming and laying in the bed with me instead of laying on the couch, but I was unable to touch her. This would drive me crazy, as my hormones would want her sexually. There I was, lying in bed sad, mad, hard, and horny, and she would act as if I weren't even there until I would cross the line. She would push me away or create even further distance. I put up with this for about three weeks to a month then something had to change. I was mentally destroying myself. All I could imagine is someone else touching or kissing her and she embraces it. This caused me to become even more upset and my thoughts would just become eviler. She was playing mind games and had mind control. I had to do something. Even if it went against what I believed in, but first I needed to try to fix it, and who better to help me fix my problems than God.

After a month I was helpless. Praying daily that my wife would come back home. I was at church three times a week, just trying not to lose hope or do anything that she would use as an excuse not to come back home. I was begging for Jesus's forgiveness, but most importantly for a miracle. Paying tithes, not listening to secular music, just trying to create a shift in energy. My last bit of hope was getting the pastor involved. Dr. Fowler was highly respected in our household, and his opinion carried weight in our home. I approached him pouring my heart out. Telling him everything that had gone on and how I felt. He planned to schedule a couples counseling session with Tiffany and I to get a better understanding and see where our minds were. He contacted her and she agreed to the meeting— this became highly anticipated by me, it was an opportunity for me to pour my heart out, explain my actions, and beg her for her forgiveness. I wanted them to know all the changes I had been making over the past year, and how I was no longer the person I was when I made my mistakes. I was on a new path, a path of less destruction, and less selfish. As the day approached, I ran many scenarios through my head. In the end, I knew I just wanted to speak from the heart and acknowledge all that I felt.

On the day of the counseling, we arrived in separate vehicles. She arrived before me. As I pulled up, I seen her car in the parking lot parked next to the church. We met in the pastor's office filled with books and Bible. Pastor Fowler was sitting relaxed in an Under-Armor sweatshirt and sweats as if he were headed to the gym after. Tiffany was dressed in business attire and appeared as beautiful as always. As we sat, we broke the ice, and the pastor began to ask us questions. The first thing he asked was if we loved one another individually. We both said yes without a doubt, but Tiffany's yes was more like a yes, I'll always love him, but being in love no. I was shocked. The pastor put focused on that statement and had her elaborate. She did so by explaining she had never felt this way, and that she never would have if I never cheated. She explained how hurt she was, how she felt betrayed, what the psychic had said, and what I had admitted to. She also said she had interest in someone else and blamed their communication on me. Saying she never even paid attention or even looked at another man until she found out I had cheated. This made me feel even less of a man, because she always looked at me as if I were all she desired. Now, it was apparent that that was no longer the case. The Pastor then asked me how I felt, and I responded by pouring out my broken heart. I started by saying how much I missed her and was sorry for my previous actions, which led us to this point. I took all accountability for what was happening, and I just wanted her to come home so we can fix it. When pastor asked Tiffany if she was willing to fix it, she gave a firm and immediate, NO! Whatever path she was on, she was determined to see what would transpire from it. At some point, she began to hold back her true feelings about her other situation, but it was only to protect my feelings. We discussed God and marriage, and she was willing to deal with all the consequences of her decisions no matter the outcome. I was devastated. The pastor was so puzzled by her statement that he recommended that we go seek professional marriage counseling, but Tiffany had no interest in the idea. She knew what she wanted, and her heart was set. Before leaving, the pastor could see the pain on my face and asked me to stay behind as Tiffany left. He offered me his guidance whenever needed and gave me his personal cell number. He prayed for me and my strength and assured me things would get better with or without Tiffany. He told me it was time to focus on myself, my children, and my relationship with God. I walked out of the church with a broken heart, hurt, and hopeless. I needed to find a way to ease this pain and to move on from this chapter. I got in my car prayed, asking God to see me through this, and not allow me to give up on this life, as I lost all hope and desire to continue.

10

HELPLESS

As I drove home, Usher's "You don't have to call," came on over the radio. As I listened to the lyrics, I felt each one as I sang loud and proudly trying to inspire and encourage myself. I needed to figure out a way to ease the pain I was feeling so I went searching through my DM. There was a lot of messages that I was yet to respond to. Many women who offered encouragement as they were aware of Tiffany and I separating. Many were women that I had already knew, and a couple were women I had yet to meet. I knew I wouldn't be lonely, but on this Christian walk could I remain celibate and deny my fleshly desires? According to my zodiac description, I have very strong sexual desires. With where I was on my walk, I now feared the exact thing that put me in this situation in the first place. And the way Tiffany was acting, she wasn't giving me any hope. That's not what's important, but it was what was on my mind. I needed to be focused on childcare, sharing custody and the days, my new budget, work, and my health. I wasn't though, all I could think about was Tiffany and what she was doing, who she was with, and what they could be doing. The mind is a powerful place when you can't control your thoughts. The vision and thought of my wife pleasuring another man, made me feel rage and jealousy inside. My mind would create visions of things I never wanted to see. Even though Tiffany and I had our experiences, it always involved only women. I love her too much to share her. It's enough that I share her with the children, but what's sacred is mine, and when it comes to her, I am selfish. So, thoughts of her spending time and giving her energy to another man killed me!

This sadness brought on so much depression that I began to get used to it. I was constantly praying to Jesus for forgiveness, but I never felt forgiven. I began to believe that I was destined to suffer, but if I were doing what God wanted me to do, why would he want me to suffer? I read it in the Bible that I was forgiven, but that wasn't my reality. The reality of it was, I was losing what meant most to me, and that was my family. The thing that I have built my legacy around. My family has always been my foundation. Now, that foundation is destroyed, and I felt as if I had nothing to stand on. These people inspired me daily to do my best and press forward. Not seeing them every day was getting to me as well, but sometimes, you have to pick your poison. This is another part of the separation that I hate. It causes you to make decisions that you do not want to make. She would take advantage of the love that I had for my family and children. She would have me keep them, but it would feel more like I was watching them so that she could date "This dude," and fuck that, I have too much pride to allow something like that to happen. There would be times she would ask me to keep the kids longer. Then when I would call, she wouldn't answer the phone. Then, I would text and not get a response. Then I'm looking and feeling stupid calling her phone repeatedly, looking like a straight stalker, but I didn't realize it. I was deep in my feelings and living in my mind. My mind would create scenarios of visions that I didn't want to see. I would hear moaning, and feel compassion slipping away from my being. I would feel anger and betrayal. My anxiety raising as I was trying to escape the rabbit hole that continued to get deeper. The further in thought that I allowed my mind to create. Searching for a feeling of pain that causes depression.

Somehow, I needed a way to fight these feelings and not allow my mind to take over. I was proud of myself in the first place for recognizing what I had been thinking. Praying to Jesus wasn't working, but it was keeping me from jumping off a ledge. The church was very supportive of my situation and there was always a brother or sister reaching out. Plus, I loved Dr. Fowler, because if I called, he would always answer and if he didn't, he would call back. This meant so much to me as he was a very popular man with a big congregation. Not to mention, he believed in me. He believed in me enough that he allowed me to deliver a message in front of the entire congregation, and I definitely accepted the offer. Out of the speeches I've ever given this one was the most nervous I have ever been still to this day. This one was an opportunity manifested extremely quickly. After reading so much of the Bible and learning so much, I wanted an opportunity to deliver the message I had received from the entire book, and the opportunity was to take place in front of the congregation. What was worse or maybe better depending on the emotion? I was definitely in despair, but I was faithful to Jesus. I figured I would tap into that spirit in order to deliver the message. As a speaker, I find myself more superficial when teaching the Gospel. The words came more from the book, and I feel as if I'm a teacher— but when I speak from the gut, I break the mind and wisdom, along with the experience and spirit. Especially if my intentions are pure, as they were, and my message was regarding making a decision and a commitment. Depending on a person's mindset, I believe this is the only way to become a great Christian. They also must have faith. You must believe in Jesus, commit to Jesus, and have faith that there is a Jesus. The more I suffered, the more I questioned. The more I questioned, the more I found a reason to suffer. My mind was driving me crazy. I truly felt the me, myself, and I within.

I was tapped in, and the day of the speech, which was on a Thursday, the church had a packed house. All the Deacons were present, and so was the Pastor and everyone who supported him. I was not only chosen to speak, but I and the Men's ministry was also involved with the entire process of the entire service. We chose the music, the performance, the headlining pastor, the announcements, the time of offering, and every other portion of the service. I sat in the audience and observed the vision manifest and it all came together. I sang, I danced, and shouted with inspiration until my name was called. I knew I was after the choir, which was purposely placed there to ignite the feeling within. I wanted to inspire the crowd to make the changes needed to reach their goals. I wanted them to know we were and still are Kings on foreign land, but I wanted them to understand that they were giving that away by the decision they were making. When I first walked up to the stage, they turned me towards another mic off to the right of the stage. I thought to myself, this sucks. Why couldn't I be in the pulpit at that fancy glass lectern, with the choir behind me? I guess I wasn't ready for that privilege, and there must be some type of system I had to get through in order to get there. Whatever it was, I shook off the thought. As I walked to the smaller lectern, I placed the notes I had written a night before on the surface. I didn't expect that I needed them, but if I did, they were there. I had seen some preachers read their entire sermon, leaving me and the rest of the crowd in utter disappointment. Anyone can write a speech and read it into a mic. I need to see that spirit come out of you. I need to hear your words and know how they feel to you. That type of speaking is boring. So, I made a vow that I would never be that type of speaker. Unless I am paid or asked to in order to deliver a direct message. As I turned towards the crowd there were men, women, and children, and none of them belonged to me. I gazed harder trying to identify someone there to support me, but there was no one.

My mind had to shift quickly, and although, I felt even more pain, the thought that I was here to deliver God's message was the motivation to proceed. After my introduction all the nerves disappeared slowly, and as I delivered my message, I could feel something takeover me. I choose to trust and not fight it, it felt as if all cylinders were ignited. The words began to flow, and the thoughts were clear. The crowd reacted; in the black church you get immediate feedback. If they like what you're saying you get a "Hallelujah", "Amen", "That's right", or a "Say it." If they are not feeling what you're saying, you won't hear anything. It seems like that when the babies start crying too, but I didn't need to worry about that. The crowd received my message well, and in the end, I received a standing ovation. This wasn't my first time speaking in front of a church, but this was my biggest experience speaking in front of the congregation and in front of the men I looked up to. When I was finished, I glanced over at the pastor and received the nod of approval. Another proud moment for me, as he entrusted me to address his flock. As I walked back to my seat, I sat there feeling accomplished. Just waiting for my mind to find a thought to take the feeling away, but the more I praised the more I distracted my mind, and I left there on a high. When I got into my car, I couldn't wait to call someone and tell them about the experience, but as I went through my call log and phone book, there was no one that I wanted to share the experience with. I mean I had people to call, but no one to help me capture the memory, or the feeling of excitement. No one who understood my journey and knew what I had been through. So, I just posted about it on Facebook and kept it pushing. What is loneliness? Having no one to share your accomplishments with. So, you talk to God. I was talking to God, but God wasn't talking back. So, I prayed for God to send me someone to talk to. Not to fall in love with, just someone to talk to.

This allowed my mind to be open to meeting new people. I immediately learned that being single in your 30's is a whole new world filled with games. When we were younger it seemed like us men were the aggressors and always horny, but when you're in your 30's woman take the title by far. Sex is everywhere and easily accessible, and there is an entire niche for single and lonely. Just check out some of these dating apps and the amount of paying members they have with yearly subscriptions. For the most part, people just want someone to talk to, but chemistry and attractiveness easily push that line. My first connection was with this Filipino single mom who had two sons. Both still young boys and she had split custody. She was a great woman and mother. She had great conversational skills, and was an excellent listener, but she was always horny and wanted to talk about sex. This girl was a straight freak, and I was in the church though, so this created a dilemma for me. We met online initially and talked a lot there before exchanging numbers. She was beautiful and took pictures showing her voluptuous breast. She had recently ended a relationship as well but had been dating for a while. She was a pro at communication, constantly staying relevant. She was interested in my well-being mentally and physically. Waking me up to a good morning text and wishing me a good night. She kept herself on my mind. We became really good friends and would talk for long periods, sometimes even for hours. During these conversations, I would learn so much. It's crazy how much a person is willing to bend for another and constantly take another's crap. From the outside looking in, you can easily see the person being played, but the person being played is completely blind and oblivious to the situation. This girl was sweet but choose to be a dummy. She knew this, but a good dick to a nymphomaniac is like a river of gold. This is where I learned dick control and didn't take this power for granted. I needed to be very careful with this superpower, so I chose to remain celibate as long as I could. I enjoyed the cat and mouse chase of the lonely and looking. I was in contact with my mother often around this time, and during our conversations, she had let me know about an old family friend from California who was now living in Las Vegas on a temporary work assignment as a nurse. She talked about how sweet she was, and how she invited my mother over for a prepared dinner. My mom also spoke highly of all her accomplishments being a college graduate and professional. She also made sure that she mentioned she really had no friends in Las Vegas and complained about being lonely. Over a conversation with my mother, she suggested that she and I meet. Curious I searched her FB profile, and although she was attractive, there was something that drew me in. There was something about her that made me want to get to know her. She was powerful, successful, intelligent, and hood, but knew how to control it. Reminding me of myself being that we were raised in the same city, went to the same schools, but she was older. My mother passed me her number, and one lonely night I decided to call. Our initial conversation was good as we filled each other out. We learned a lot about each other over a 40-minute conversation. We began to talk frequently and the more we talked the longer the duration. We began to talk so much that we filled each other's break times. Not just the break times while working, but also the lunchtimes. Then that grew to travel time, before bedtime, and good mornings. This became overwhelming as my mind wasn't ready for all this. I created a controversy with her regarding religion and created some distance. At this time, I am a devout Christian and she practices Ancestor Worship. I made this out to be a huge deal and identified this as a reason not to talk. Somehow though after a month of no communication, I was back texting her. Matter of fact, it was something she posted on FB. A picture wearing a sexy corset. I sure know it will attract plenty of men in the DM after that, but she was responsive to me. We caught up with one another and the situations were technically the same. She had met some guy at work, a Corrections Officer. As for me, I was talking to the Filipino chick and things were becoming interesting. With her, I knew the physical attraction was there, because during our first meet up at the bar. During most of our conversation, I tried to stay a gentleman with my dick hard 90% of the night.

Even knowing what I was capable of I fought it off and didn't give in. Deep down I knew I would eventually, but I wanted God to see my efforts, plus I still had hope of Tiffany coming home.

Although, this was all so overwhelming. It distracted my mind from pain and despair. I had one woman rejecting me, another one pouring into me, and another helping me to grow and feeding my soul. Cali and I had amazing conversations. We talked from a place of spirit, deep conversations, soul to soul. This intrigued me about her more than anything, I appreciated her mind and perspectives. With the Filipino woman, she was genuine and sweet. She had a heart of gold and was fun. Constantly making me laugh— even came to workout with me a few times. We did dinner, lunch, and even went out for my best friend Theo's birthday. Matter of fact that night she was my date and we danced all night. Wearing a little black dress and heels made her the perfect height for dance floor groping. She kept me excited, especially when she told me she wasn't wearing any panties. I imagine you could see the scene vividly if you could imagine a female dog in heat wag her ass in front of the male dog, and the male dog going crazy. I know my male dog used to lose his mind when the female dog would go in heat. It was like he could smell the pheromones from a mile away. I knew that night I was going to give in and get it. I had held back for far too long.

Plus, I had found out that Tiffany was going to California with the dude for a photo shoot. To me, that meant the worse, so I was like screw fighting it. It's time to do me. I had to protect my Ego, a matter of fact it was time to bring him back. So that's what I was on. Some revenge type, player type that will protect my heart through sex shit, and after a few drinks I was like fuck it. We went back to my place where her car was parked. We chilled in the garage and talked for a minute. One thing led to another and we are discussing condoms. We had a great night, and the days following you would have thought we would be closer, but after talking a few times. It was crazy how my mind shifted to Cali. I honestly have no idea what had taken place with me mentally, but I was craving something else, and I was already intrigued, and it hadn't died out yet.

My new focus was Cali. We connected by phone again and decided to stop playing on the phone and meet for once. She came over after her shift late one night. We had been texting all day, and I just threw it out there, that I wanted to feed her after she got off. It was super late like midnight, so I just bought us some Del Taco. That night we talked for hours. That night I was back to my old ways, but this girl had me stuck. Our friendship and bond was super dope. We educated each other, understood each other children, respected each other's beliefs, and she was a freak. Not the most attractive in person, but she was seductive. She had my mind, my body, and she was coming for my soul.

As Cali and I became closer she became more vocal. She was strong-minded and respected herself to the fullest. Very intelligent and recognized things before they occurred, and her intuition was always spot on. One quality I disliked was how controversial she was. Every discomfort was a blow-up or argument. Our first argument was one of my family pictures still being on the wall that included Tiffany. She said, "Every time I come over and walk past these pictures, I feel weird. It's like she is watching me. Take those pictures down or I'm never coming back over here again." What could I say, she had a point, and I never really thought anything of it. I just didn't want my kids to feel any different. After a few weeks, what seemed like a game to them then became reality, and they were feeling the effects of family separation. They were hurting, their life was now inconvenienced. Rules were different, and both parents are hurt and depressed. I hated seeing my children suffer. Cali had kids as well who had been suffering themselves. Not having a two-parent home is destroying the future of families for generations to come. For some people, they become successful and they overcome the odds, but many make a wrong turn at some point and never get back on track or realize it too late. These kids were brilliant children, but they were hurting inside. Sensitive to this world that is full of destruction. Caught up in vanity, and the need for power. Super talented children, and would teach me so much about life, decisions, personalities, and deception. Broken families are hurting. Someone somewhere is suffering.

The children came home to empty walls and asked immediately. "Daddy where are all the pictures?" I said "I took them down, babies. Mommy doesn't see us as a family anymore and neither should we." Brazyl says, "Mommy isn't coming back?" I say, no time soon." The kids went upstairs crying— they hated this situation now. Going to mommy's house was no longer a sleepover, and Cali put a stop to Tiffany watching the kids at the house too. Things had changed. Tiffany had realized now that letting go of the family was starting to drift completely away. I was focused on healing and creating a family environment around me. Cali and I were growing closer. She was speaking life into me daily. She knew the days I would feel depressed about my situation and would snap me out of it quick. She would dance, sing, pray, whatever to change the way I feel. It was like she had superpowers. The real talk is that she has the power to heal or destroy, and I have witnessed this on command. Dealing with her, I would need to develop a strength within myself like no other, plus I would need to stay faithful. Women like that can put curses on your life. All her former boyfriends and baby daddies were suffering in some way. Even her most successful one had lost his fame and power— he would miss out on the rise of the black community movement. A movement he once led. Others were in jail, so the outcome of separation with her was destruction. By the time I realized this, I was into deep. Cali fell in love quickly and got attached. Although, it was weird, it became comforting. When Tiffany left me that took a lot away from my self-confidence. I was once maybe overly confident, and I felt the exact opposite. This must be how she felt after my infidelities? I began to realize. I played myself, but before falling into depression Cali was there. She became my drug. Open to discover new things and share moments of life with me. When no one was there for my birthday that year, she was. When I told her I wanted to go hiking, she said, "Let's do it." We then went and bought hiking shoes and lunch. I packed our backpacks and went hiking for five hours. We talked about life and joked. Creating an even stronger bond and connecting. Another thing I had admired about her was her ability to make me smile. She joked a lot and sang. Always with the right energy to create happiness. She was attentive to my thoughts and feelings and encouraged my success. This was the energy that I needed around me. This was the energy of healing. As our bond got stronger, I felt a sort of healing. I developed a love for Cali that was awkward. It was as if I owed her a part of me. I began to feel as if I needed her as well. She was smart and she was aware of my separation situation and child custody. She knew of all that was happening in my life. I was transparent with her, and she began to realize Tiffany's games and predicted her moves. Which gave me more clarity and a strategic approach.

One thing I learned during this time was the power of removing emotions out of situations, especially with certain people. Many times, they are battling their hurt and taking out their pain on others. I had to develop the mentality that I will not be your victim, and you will not control the way I feel. The war I was fighting was psychological and if I was levelheaded, I was strong. So, I learned to master removing my emotions out of situations and listening to what the person is telling me about themselves and what they are experiencing in their mind. In this way, I know how to properly react to a situation for the benefit of all the parties, and not allow emotions to cause me to act on impulse. I know how to control myself when I need to.

In the next couple of months, things transpired in my life that felt clearly out of my control and changed the way I see life, and the power of reciprocity. I was feeling happier and stronger, but on the inside, I was empty. Every day there were these moments that I would get depressed, but I would smoke weed and snap out of it. Some weed would make you think and feel more emotions than others, but I learned to use it as a tool. Weed would help me with my focus but would affect my memory. This for me was the perfect recipe for dealing with my depression. What was even better was Cali smoked too. So, those conversations were on another level. We would discuss our dreams, in which she had many, but the one she fixed on was a nursing position she applied for in Florida, and how their recruiting had been in contact with her after six months of waiting. She had plans of staying in a high-rise on the beach and practicing her Ifa religion with the heavy population who practice

Santeria. An Afro/Cuban religion that originated in Yoruba. This move would mean so much to her on her development of evolution. So, she was ecstatic when she got the email and job offer. I was able to experience her joy because I was the first person she called with the great news. I was happy for her and although I was able to smile, I began to worry. I asked, "When do they plan on you transferring?" She replied, "In three weeks." I was devastated. She was my healing. My source of happiness, and the only person I could be myself with and talk to. Plus, my intimacy partner at the time. Now, she was just up and leaving, that hurt. I was thinking about how I would be going right back to lonely and probably connecting with the Filipino woman again. The good thing is I would be able to focus more on church and get myself together. The days leading up to her leaving we made all the prior arrangements. We made reservations and she received her assignment, but first, she needed to consult with her Babalawo (Ifa Priest). She did just that and I'm not sure what came out in the consultation, but she was told to go to the store and buy these items. Rum, fruit, honey, molasses, candles, herbs, amongst other things. She was told to drive to the lake and throw the items inside. Cali had never been to the lake and asked me if I could take her and her children. I didn't mind and the following weekend afternoon we prepared by buying all items, wearing all white, and drove to the lake. We found a spot in private and as I watched she went into the lake and began to pray and sing. The way her colorful beads looked on her brown skin while she wore all white was powerfully beautiful. It was amazing witnessing her practice African culture. Something that had been stripped from my ancestors to the point that I never even knew it existed. And now, it right before me. I was intrigued. The entire moment appeared taboo, but it felt right. It was an amazing sight. Enough to be inspired and partake in the ceremony. Leaving the lake that day, I'm not sure exactly what happened, but the events that followed were divine. My life again will never be the same.

11

FACEBOOK STATUS: IT'S COMPLICATED

U p to this point, I had been going to church three times a week, trying to find my salvation repeatedly. Mentally I had found myself suffering realizing that it was psychological. I was filled with guilt, anger, and of course resentment. I prayed often talking to God. Hoping that the next day would be better. I also read and studied the Bible daily, but the desire to go to church had suddenly escaped me. There was a time before this that I wouldn't miss church, Bible studies, or any of the classes— but suddenly that love and desire changed. I began to want to learn more and more about Ifa. I knew it was the time on the lake that did this. I needed to know why I felt this change of heart, and the only way for me to do so was research, which was quite easy to do as it was my escape from my feelings and took me on a search. The research takes you on an adventure, searching for a reliable sources and information, I never knew existed. Opening to a new world of knowledge, understanding, and spirituality. I've witnessed things that would make me sound crazy if I discussed them with people who don't understand. I've been introduced to a community of people that I never even noticed although all the signs were present. Studying something new was just what I needed. I personally needed to cleanse my spirit and mind of its original programming, and discover a new code, but first, it was time to go through some mess.

The year 2016 was definitely one of the most trying times of my life. The fourth quarter itself provided too many days that felt like survival, as I was at mental war with myself and others, physically and spiritually. I was living a life that I hated and was constantly faced with dilemmas and decisions of right and wrong, good or evil, and facing the consequences. I felt like I knew too much, while dealing with emotions, but had no self-control. My mind was constantly wondering what Tiffany was doing. Whether she had the kids or not, and this affected my relationship. For the most part, I think I was able to hide it, but knowing Cali she knew what was really up. Around this time, I believe Tiffany was trying to get revenge— her intentions were for me to experience pain. She knew exactly what to do and say in order to irritate my spirit. I monitored her social media, in which she was very private not really posting much, but then she would do some shady shit, like post a model picture of her new boyfriend on our daughter's fan page marketing his personal brand. Although, we were not friends, she knew I had access to that page and would see it. Another time was when she went out to dinner with a mutual friend, introducing her new boyfriend, taking photos, and the friend posting them on her FB, where of course, I could see, or the moments where we would have to come together and do an interview on the news together to promote Brazyl's safety event, and not even talk to each other. Go to events together and have our new flings stay at home while we worked together, staying as far away from each other as possible. Usually, finding a way to get irritated with one another and hating each other even more.

What really hurt about this time and made it extremely emotional was the fact that we were going through these problems during the holidays. Being what I consider a family man, the holidays means so much to us. It's a time where the trend is family focus and enjoyment. Everything is happiness and jolly, but when the emotions don't match the energy of the world, it can cause depression. Untreated depression causes life around you to fall apart, while the life inside you becomes destructive or dormant. I spent thanksgiving with my mom's side of the family. Many of us got together that day at my Uncle Gene's house. Although we were having a good time, family conversations began to become personal and my separation was a hot topic. Many family members were supportive and offered words of encouragement, but my uncle Gene was on one. Gene became tremendously rude and insensitive, and made fun of my situation in front of the family. He had his negative remarks about the separation and my decision making, but what caught me by surprise was when he was having a conversation about my cousin. The conversation came up that his son was raising someone else's son, while the son doesn't know that he is not his biological father. This caused a big commotion amongst the family. Then, he proceeded to look at me and said, "Same goes for you, you niggas are fools for living that life and raising those kids like that." I was livid. I stared him deep in his eyes and held back my words. I stood up and walked away while the family argued with Gene over the shit he had just said. I walked into Gene's garage, lit the blunt, and meditated on what Gene had said. I contemplated violence, disrespect, and destroying the entire function. I then thought about what he said as he had opened one of my most sensitive healed wounds ever. My firstborn son.

You see, all my life I have had my doubts about my junior due to the way Tiffany and I starting off our relationship. She had just stopped a relationship a couple of weeks prior. When we reconnected hot and heavy from the start. It was me and her every day, six weeks later, we found out we she was pregnant. Even though I felt this, I've never wanted to disrupt the peace and narrative. For this conversation to have come up in front of the family made me feel like a complete fool, and if this is true then I have been living a lie for 12 years. I could hear Gene in the living room still making remarks and discussing features and comparisons to mine. I got even more upset, walked in on the conversation, and asked Gene to come to talk to me in the room. He got up and strutted in the room walking confidently in the room without a care in the world. As we entered the room I closed the door behind us, before he could turn around to sit down on the bed, I took out a crowbar and whacked it across his head knocking him to the floor unconscious. I then took the sharp part of the crowbar and shoved it through his skull over and over leaving blood everywhere. Just kidding, I definitely thought of it though. What I did do was approached him like a man with respect. I told him how I felt and discussed with him what I was experiencing in life at that time. He did what most people do and started comparing my experience to one of his similar experiences in the past, when he was fighting for custody of his son. After telling me the story, he was able to revisit the feelings I was experiencing and apologized for what he had said. We continued with the day and had a much better time, but what he said about my son would not leave my mind. The thought was heavy. I needed someone to talk to, but who. Who could I have a non-biased discussion with that I could trust and listen? After I left there the anger increased and I called the one person who was always there, Cali. I told her exactly how I felt. I told her the entire story.

You see Tiffany and I met in San Bernardino while attending high school. We knew of each other, but never made a connection. During my senior in school, I left California and moved to Las Vegas with my grandmother. I graduated in 2002 at the age of 17 and after graduation, I was on my own. In 2004 while at the strip club, I ran into Tiffany here in Las Vegas. We recognized one another and made an instant connection. We were limited in our interaction due to her being in a relationship with a guy in the Air Force. After a few weeks though and a few conversations in between. I had visited the club weekly, just to see her and spend whatever time she would allow. There was one weekend I went to see her at the club and she wasn't there. I called her to see if she was coming in that night and she said no. I told her I had only come to see her. That's when she invited me over. Excited, I accepted the invite and went over with no intention of doing anything physical. I honestly was going over just to kick it and talk. I arrived 30 minutes later, from the invite to a small studio apartment complex behind the strip. I knock on the studio door and Tiffany answers wearing SpongeBob pajamas. Obviously, she wasn't intending on anything physical either. That night we talked for hours and the later it got the more tired I was getting, so I asked to crash on her couch for a few hours to get some rest before going home. She agreed and gave me a pillow and sheet. After laying on the couch for 15 minutes I had experienced some of the most uncomfortable resting I had ever, so I decided to lay on the floor. Tiffany must have felt pity, so she invited me to lay in the bed. I accepted, one thing led to another, and we were inseparable nearly every day after. Having sexcapades daily. A month later she told me she was pregnant. At that point, I had no doubts, because although I was pulling out, I wasn't using protection. What was crazy at this time was there was another woman that I was infatuated with as well that was a former co-worker at the resort I was working as a lifeguard at that time. All the time I had known her she had a partner, and after her latest breakup, she was finally giving me the time and action I always wanted. We also had created a bond and the days I didn't see Tiffany; I would see her. We were not physical much, but the couple times we were, I remember slipping up while she was on top of me. The shit was intense, and she too was pregnant at the same time as Tiffany. This was my first real-life dilemma, and after a few months she knew about Tiffany, but Tiffany didn't know about her. She told me to decide who I was going to be with, I choose Tiffany, and a week later she had an abortion. Although that made the situation easy that I was dealing with, she completely stopped talking to me, and the fact that she went through that alone without me bothered me. I had never felt a pain of guilt like that before, and we kind of ghosted one another. After that decision was made, I owed it to Tiffany and the baby, now born (Brandon Jr) the best life that I could provide. At the hospital, my family voiced to me their concern and I spoke with Tiffany. She told me if I had any doubts to get a DNA test and confirmed me that once she had been intimate with me, it was only me. I loved her so much I declined the test. I made that vow when I asked God to give me a boy. I remember praying and saying I vowed to be the best father I possibly could and would raise him to be an amazing man. Once Tiffany got the ultrasound and it announced boy, I was all in. The reason for me dropping out of college and quit my dream of playing baseball and becoming a police officer at the age of 22. For 12- years I had been raising BJ. During the 12 years the signs were there, but why disrupt a family's complete lively hood. A marriage, a career, and a second child three years later. I was committed, but there were always these reminders that BJ and I had no connection.

We had so many differences, you would think we were of different ethnic spectrums. I'm not saying all kids are like their parents, but there are many underlying similarities that can't be avoided. Something, as small as a smile or a temper can be passed down genetically. We've never really shared much. There have been times I've felt doubts and studies our photos. My current and his current photo. My baby and his baby photo, and never had I found anything that stood out. These thoughts were usually inspired by my mother who always had doubts. The situation has become so heated that we have stopped talking for years, because she too believes my son was not my son. The thought of the truth and the pain I could possibly endure if BJ was not my biological son would be too excruciating to bear and could possibly destroy relationships for years to come. With that pushed in the back of my mind, I continued with life and never had confronted Tiffany about it. Cali listened to all that I had to say and suggested maybe it was time to find out. With all I was experiencing at the time, I just wasn't ready, but it was something that needed to be revisited in the future.

Over the next month leading up to Christmas, things began to get out of hand. Tiffany and I were not getting along at all. We were sharing custody with the children, and them being young kids they made sure they shared everything they experienced. It didn't take long for the kids to tell me that Mommy had a new boyfriend with a long beard. My youngest daughter Berlyn said she liked to play and put stickers in it. Of course, this led me to asking additional questions that I shouldn't have. But these are my kids, and I want to know 100% about their life and who they are exposed to. I wanted to know how much time he was spending there and told them not to ever sit on any man's lap. I asked where they slept, they said the bed when it's just Mommy, and Mommy slept in the living room when her boyfriend was there. Although, I didn't care this bothered me. After a couple of weeks, they said he was always there. After questioning Tiffany, she confirmed that it was the same guy who her co-worker and I was had talked to that night in June.

This made me distance my heart even more, which created pain, and every time I was experiencing pain Cali was there to heal me. This made me fall for her even more. Not only did she listen and have understanding she gave advice. The way she was raised, she was super loyal. If I had a beef with someone, she had a beef with them. Especially if they are trying to hurt or harm me. She hated when Tiffany would take advantage of me. She said

"Tiffany is always inconveniencing my life in order to convenience her own. That's married people shit. Isn't that the point of having a husband? She shouldn't get husband privileges with a whole another man laid up next to you, having sex with you, and playing daddy and expecting my man to help you." She continued, "That's just stupid, and you need to stop falling for her bullshit and man up. She probably with the nigga right now." She told me this while I had recently agreed to keep the kids longer in order for Tiffany to go to an interview. Brazyl had therapy, so I called off work in order to take her to the appointment. For some reason, what Cali had said was repeated in my mind, so I called Tiffany and received no answer. I decided that after the appointment I would drive by her new apartment to see if she was there. The good thing was you could see her parking spot from the street. Following the appointment, I drove by and seen the car parked in the stall. Her interviewed was scheduled for 10 am and it was 09:55 am and she was still there, or maybe she got a ride from someone else? A voice within says, "Go knock on her door."

Although, I had never been to her apartment before, I always knew where it was, because she made an order on our Amazon account and Amazon saved all the information. I pull into the apartments, park, walk to her door. I her laughing a giggling. I knock on the door and hear a man's voice say, "Are you expecting someone? A female voice replies, "No," and I stood off to the side so no one would see through the peephole. The door unlocks and the guy looks out. This is our first official time to see each other and my mind was like a bull seeing red. I invite myself in the apartment shoving through both of them and sit on the couch. By the looks of it, they were wrapping Christmas gifts. I didn't give a f*ck, she lied. They were talking shit, but I wasn't listening. I was just playing in my mind how I was going to handle the situation. A piece of me was thinking murder, but the peace in me was thinking future. I wasn't going to touch the guy, but when he got in my face trying to protect Tiffany while she was talking shit, I shoved him out of the way, and we began to wrestle. I was obviously stronger than the guy, but somehow, I lost my footing. He then picked me up as I jumped putting him in a choke hold while he slammed us through the dining room table, destroying the thing completely. I kept him in the choke hold and began to choke him out, but I would constantly release pressure. I didn't want to kill the guy, I just wanted him to feel me, and know I wasn't just about to let him take my family without him knowing in the back of his head I would one day destroy their peace this easily. Plus, I don't fight fair, if ever he would get an advantage or almost get out the headlock, I would bite him, but not enough to get through the skin. Tiffany tried to grab me, so I let him go, and left the house a complete ransack. She followed me out talking shit, and I told her, "You are going to suffer, I hope you rot bitch, for everything you're doing to this family." She replied, "you're just jealous because my nigga looks better than you and I'm about to give him everything you used to have. Matter of fact, I'm about to go suck his D right now." After I left, she followed up with a bunch of mean nasty text messages. The one that stood out said, "I'm calling the police, you better buy me a new table." She then took pictures of her apartment and sent them to me. The apartment had looked like swat had gone in there looking for drugs and guns. I was sorry but being bad felt good for the time being. I was worried, but then I wasn't. I went home, smoked a blunt, and who was there for the healing? Cali. I was becoming addicted to her. With Tiffany having the kids for Christmas, Cali thought it would be good for us to go visit our families in California. I needed a change of environment. I thought this was a great idea, but the same night following the altercation, which was December 23rd, Tiffany ended up in the hospital. She couldn't move the left side of her body, and the doctors said she had a mild stroke. I didn't find out until the next day, and Tiffany said her boyfriend was with the kids at her house. I hung up the phone and meditated on the situation. How the hell did she have a stroke? She was only 31 at the time. I know I said what I said about her suffering, but damn, like this? Cali was at home packing for our trip, when I called her and told her, I could hear the anger in her voice. I drove to her house to let her know I needed to adjust the plans or cancel them, because Tiffany was in the hospital. When I got to the house, she was in the bathroom putting on makeup. I went to hug her, and she said, "Don't touch me."

I asked, "Why?"

And she said, "You are a weak ass nigga, a fucking pussy, who deserves everything that's happening to you. You deserved for your wife to leave you. I hate you; I hope you fucking die. You know what, just kill yourself, I never want to see you again." She said violently. I was shocked and had no idea how to react. All I did was call an Uber to come get me, and I got out of there. I was crushed. I had to get it together though because I needed to get my children. I was going to go pick up the kids from Tiffany's boyfriend, but that would have been dumb. I was already on 10 with my anger and the sight of seeing the man I had just got into an altercation with, would be a lose-lose situation. I went home to prepare the house for the kids for the holiday weekend. While there, Cali pulls up and apologizes for what she said before leaving for California. I didn't care what she said at that point. I was cutting her off and never wanted to see or talk to her again. She tried everything in the book to try to get me to respond to her, but my mind was focused on getting my children, Tiffany being in the hospital, my crazy altercation with her boyfriend, and what I needed to do next. I had never had someone talk to me like that before, and never had I come so close to hitting a woman. I needed to step away. Cali tried to convince me to bring the kids with us, but I passed. After so many failed attempts she left and went to California. Tiffany decided in order to keep the peace, it would be best to have me meet her and the kids in her hospital room where she was receiving treatment and her boyfriend would be there.

As odd as it felt, I followed with what needed to be done to get my children. We met in the hospital room and Tiffany went live on FB while the kids opened their gifts in the room and the Santa actor there as well. Her boyfriend was fully engaged with the kids which got my respect, but by Tiffany going live on FB, it made me feel and look like a sucker. I got out of there as soon as I could and took the kids home.

That evening I would ignore all calls from Cali and text, until she sent one of a positive pregnancy test. This caught me completely by surprise as I thought "Not again." I called her immediately and asked WTF. She said she was late and decided to take a test. That was why she responded the way she did in the bathroom when she yelled. She didn't know how to deal with the emotions and flipped out. I was shocked, I couldn't believe this was happening again, and now with a monster. I was speechless and got off the phone. The next day, was Christmas and Tiffany wanted to see the children. I took them to the hospital to visit. Tiffany could tell there was a lot on my mind. She asked her boyfriend and the kids to step out while we talked. For some reason, at that moment I wanted to share the news that was on my mind. I showed her the pregnancy test and she began to cry. She was so hurt, and I didn't understand why, but I liked it. After what she was putting me through, I loved seeing her suffer.

With Tiffany in the hospital, I had the kids longer. This was a plus, but horrible timing. For some reason, the home Cali was renting was being foreclosed and she received an eviction notice. With three weeks to find a place, she was unable to, and my dumb ass at the time invited her and her family to move into my house until she found a place to stay. This was a horrible idea and the details of it I plan to write in its own book itself. This is catastrophic to every party involved. I strongly disagree with this, but hey that's because I experienced it, and it sucks. After a couple of weeks, Cali had her period and we discovered she wasn't pregnant. I never told Tiffany this, but with her thinking Cali was pregnant she was showing her cards. For a person who no longer loved me or wanted to be with me, she was deeply in her emotions. There was a constant back and forth between the both, and it was driving me crazy. I was losing myself. Always stressed, surrounded by negative energy daily. Always overwhelmed and angry daily but having to suppress the feelings because my words cause a damage. I was lost, depressed, angry, sad, disappointed, embarrassed, broke, and dying. Things continued to get worse, especially when Tiffany moved in with her boyfriend and filed for cash aid, which caused the state to charge me for child support. I then filed for a divorce and opened Pandora's Box.

With all the pain I was feeling I figured it was the perfect time to explore all my demons. I became transparent with everything in my life and wanted to face it all. I had been experiencing so much pain that it could not get any worse. I was at the point of numbness and giving up was an option. It was time for justice and justification. I stopped talking to Tiffany completely for a couple of months. During this time, I purchased a home DNA test kit from Walgreens. BJ and I took the test and sent it to the lab for results. The box said it would take four to six weeks to receive the results. I wanted them electronically to expedite the process. The anticipation of the results was intense. I smoked so much that month. I was so scared; the truth would finally be known and what I always felt would be truthful or deceiving. I checked my email every day, just hoping they would under promise and over-deliver. BJ asked about the test, but I told him it was just something for the dentist. I told him something boring so he wouldn't tell his mom.

After approximately five weeks passed, I one day woke up to a new email. I knew this was it. Before opening it, I walked downstairs into the home office while everyone was still asleep. I prayed to myself that whatever the result, allow me to be strong and react appropriately. That gave me a little more courage and I proceeded to open this email that confirmed that I was not BJ's biological father. I was crushed... Now, I thought the pain of losing my grandma, not making it in baseball, losing my career, Brazyl's accident, and losing my family was bad. This one right here was the icing on the cake. 12 years of sacrifice. I stopped going to college and playing baseball for this boy. I got married and a career for this boy. I accelerated my adulthood to provide for him, and he isn't mine. I sacrificed a relationship with my mother, and one worse aborted a baby I knew was mine for them and he isn't my son. This pain ran deep, so deep that I just wanted to get away and leave everything. Fly to another country and never come back. I was destroyed. I sent the email to her sister and her mother. They were the two people I was in constant contact on her side of the family. I then told Tiffany, and she didn't believe me. I said how the f*ck don't you believe me? Why would I lie about something like this?" She replied, this is fake, and you be ashamed of yourself for doing this. She picked up BJ and he never came over again.

The next few months were straight out of hell. My life was miserable. My girls hated coming to my house, because of Cali's family, and this created a divide. My daughters always loved being with me but started to want to stay with their mom. You see Cali became very violent at times, physically assaulting me in ways that if I retaliated would ruin my future and sacrifice my freedom. This was to the point where my daughters witnessed it and also seen her spacing out foaming at the mouth as if she was the poltergeist. Shit was getting crazy. I was dealing with baby daddies trying to jump me, another baby daddy pulls a gun on me, and another baby daddy that was really an attached ex. I hated my life so much. Every day I had to meditate, walk, read, and smoke. Every day I had to separate myself from the world, but at no point was I going to give up on myself. I had too much responsibility. I have too many people depending on me. I have too many talents that need to be explored and given.

12

LESSONS

The power of prayer and forgiveness is strong, but as I have said before it takes time to heal. Speaking of prayer, be careful what you pray for, because when God/Universe moves, sometimes the result is immediate and turbulent.

October 1st, 2017 will forever be a day the city of Las Vegas will never forget. To our community of Las Vegas, this was the night Domestic Terrorism hit the Las Vegas strip and 58 people lost their lives at a Country music concert. I on the other hand will remember this day for the rest of my life, because of other reasons.

As mentioned in the previous chapter. I had a baby daddy pull a gun on me. Crazy, but true! You see the night before, Cali's son got into it with her and got into her face. Me, being the man of the house jumped up and sat him down. He then picked up a guitar drum pole and attempted to hit me while sitting down. I jumped up and pushed his face, hitting his nose and causing it to bleed. The boy was in rage until he saw blood dripping from his nose. At that point, the entire house went crazy. Which consisted of all the kids yelling at me and one taking a picture of her brother and sending it to his dad. The house was in complete unrest and chaos at this time. Through the evening I could hear the kids talking to their dad and stepdads, to the point I knew I was in for some shit. The next evening, although things were not going well, I was moving forward. The best way to deal with stress is to work on yourself. I once again was in my garage working out, listening to music, and planning my next move, when I heard a male voice yelling. Not being able to make out what he was saying, I moved forward with my set. As the male walked closer, I could see the anger on his face and that it was the boy's father. He then reached in his waist band, and I ran to the light switch and shut off the light in the garage. As I ran in the house to get my gun, I called the police. As I was on the phone with the operator, I walked back to the garage and the man was still there three houses away with his gun. At any time, I could have pulled the trigger and justified myself, but the man said to me, if you ever touch my son again, I will kill you, and ran away. I gave the operator the description and they sent units immediately. One to my house and many others casing the area, including the helicopter. While two officers stayed with me to file the report, the others continued to look for the suspect. While there, as a trained former police officer, I knew their protocol and radio codes, and was paying attention to the radio traffic. They were focused on my event until officers came over the radio looking for officer assistance throughout the valley. There was a shooting on the strip and many bodies on the floor with the suspect still anonymous. With this traffic coming over the radio, every officer on my event left and drove down to the terror. One officer stayed behind, but eventually he had to leave me to go help his colleagues. I called Tiffany told her there was an emergency and to come get the kids. She arrived immediately, taking the girls, but concerned about me after learning what had happened. She said if you need somewhere to go, come to her apartment. After going back into the house there was no way I would be able to sleep in peace. Plus, I needed to be with my kids, so I took Tiffany's offer and went to her home that night. Although it was late, we talked for hours about everything.

The next day I went back home and packed my things and moved with my Uncle Gene. This was an interesting scenario, as he had just experienced a stroke a month prior which caused him to have blurred vision. This restricted his driving and all other activities, and he needed the help. His wife was there for him, but she had no sympathy. She was always rude to him and in a bad mood. Taking notice of this energy, I could tell he was getting worse daily.

He was always depressed, sad, and angry. We had many long conversations and he had no hope for the future. I could tell because all he would talk about was the past. I have been here before, and I was determined to get him out of it. First, I let him know his value. I told him all the good qualities of himself that I noticed and the type of leader he could become. Second, we discussed goals and life mission. I wanted to know what he always desired to become. Of course, he said a professional athlete, but after doing some talking, we found out that he liked to cultivate Marijuana. Something that would keep him busy, but not cause stress at his age. We discussed much more, and as the weeks past, with some walking, listening to music, and not wasting time on negative energy. He was improving daily. I would spend my days at his home and my evenings at Tiffany's.

At Tiffany's we were forming a bond again, but we were still somewhat talking to our exes. I had lost all interest after me and Cali's breakup. The way it happened; I would be crazy to consider ever even seeing her again. After multiple attempts, she just faded away. Tiffany had control of her situation. Her ex would call and message occasionally, but to a level that was expected.

As Tiffany and I became closer, I began to spend the night. Spending more time together we dealt with issues, and as we dealt with our issues, we forgave each other. Forgiveness can be difficult, but it's necessary for our future. I have learned that when forgiving someone, it is best to let them know how bad they have hurt you, and how you may never forget what happened, but you will not hold it against them. When asking for forgiveness, the best things we can do is be truthful, sympathetic, remorseful, understanding, and stick to our word.

Tiffany and I needed time to heal, trust, and forgive. No matter how hard we tried to fake the bond and connection we shared to the world, spirit would not allow us to. But over time we became more connected, and in January 2018, Tiffany was pregnant with our 4th child. I know, crazy turn of events right. As months passed, Gene got better, and I moved back in with my family.

The Pain of a Man is his own personal battle. Depending on his mindset, the Pain will either motivate or destroy him into change. Change is the cure to all painful and stressful situations. What once was is no longer valid, nor does it serve. Pain brings disruption to reality. It is the starting point of identifying evidence of error. With further investigation you can identify the source. I say this to say we must identify the source and do whatever possible to correct it. If not, we experience trauma. Emotional and psychological trauma is the result of extraordinarily stressful events that shatter your sense of security, making you feel helpless in a dangerous world. This leads us to act out of desperation or emotion. Those actions usually result into transferred trauma, where we cause pain or trauma to someone else. And then everyone around you suffers.

I'm done suffering. Life has completely kicked my ass, but the battle is not over. Through my experiences I've learned many valuable lessons. The pain is necessary. It makes you stronger, wiser, and more in tuned with yourself. Most of all, it demands change and healing. This can be a long process but getting to know yourself takes time. Plus, we are always changing and comparing ourselves to whom we once were. For most that is a person that they never created but was influenced by society and culture. As we get older our results in life tell the truth. We learn what's working for us and what's not. Who is good for us and who is not, and it's our power to change?

One thing I know for sure is that I changed. I do not hate the man was before, but I do know he could have been better. My way with dealing with pain has always been sex. The feeling of satisfaction was a definite substitute and distraction, but when you mix sex with depression, resentment, and recklessness, sex is an action with immediate satisfaction and delayed consequences. So, I was doing myself more harm than good, and so where the people around me.

There are a few lessons I hope you take from this book.

1. The power of hope and faith. If you believe it, you can achieve it. You must believe in yourself.

2. Accept the truth for what it is and correct what you can.

3. Be sincere of others and yourself but be truthful.

4. Evaluate yourself, be honest, and seek help where you need it.

5. Learn how to communicate the good and the bad.

6. Stop running and face your problems or fears.

7. Spend time with yourself and Meditate.

8. Pray

9. Listen to uplifting and empowering messages.

10. Read positive messages.

11. Attend therapy or counseling.

12. Have a support group of people who understand what you're going through and that you trust.

13. Be patient but work on improving yourself daily.

14. Physical fitness.

15. Study, educate yourself.

16. Trust the process.

17. Know when to surrender and realize when God is in control.

18. Create a plan to get better.

19. There is an energy that is here to destroy you. It knows all your weaknesses and inadequacies. You must identify that energy, and how it attempts to entice and transform you.

20. There is an energy that is here to protect you. It knows everything about you, especially your gifts and strengths. You must learn how to tap into that energy so that you will be empowered daily and able to fight off all negative energy that is after you.

I wrote this book for the person who is going through something, getting through something, or going into something. Maybe it's just us, but you are not alone. I've faced my many trials, tribulations, and heartbreak and times where I felt too weak to give up, I found something within that would not allow me to give in. Through all adversity, I learned to change where it was needed and work on self-improvement through the healing process. This has given me a competitive edge and a superpower of strength when facing adversity. The best part of life is that you get 24 hours before the clock resets. We always have the freedom and ability to change our lives. All wounds heal, we just must be fit enough to face the process. I am stronger because of my wounds. This story has a very happy ending.

There soon will be a testimony to share.

God Bless,

13

AFTERWARD

What was once a therapeutic experience manifested into a book and many other ways to come. Getting through my mess took a lot of work. I spent many hours alone, studying, and trying to figure it out. As I worked on myself, I discovered who I was, and realized my gifts and capabilities. At some point, I found the information helpful, and I've been dying to share it with the world. Many people know my story on the surface, but not what I felt within. If you read this book in its entirety, I am truly grateful and appreciate you reading my thoughts.

I went through a lot of heartache and depression, and I truly believe I deserved it all. The people we encounter on our journey arrive for a reason and we connect with them due to the law of attraction. The energy we put into this world is what will soon return. I am conscious of my every decision at this point in my life. All I want is the good that I deserve and the ability to spread it all over the world. I want to be essential and help others. I pray this book achieved this.

I am truly grateful to those who came before me and set the path. The authors and orators such as Eric Thomas, Les Brown, Bishop TD Jakes, Dick Gregory, Eckhart Tolle, Zig Ziglar, and many more. Your work will continue

to make an impact and last forever. I am
   blessed to come across your work during the right time of my journey.

14

ACKNOWLEDGEMENTS

Special thanks to my beautiful wife Tiffany. My inspiration and Soul Mate, the past few years of life has forced us to work on forgiveness and love. Our love is destined, I am looking forward to us putting our past behind us and creating the life we always imagined for our family.

Special thanks to my hero Brazyl for showing me the true meaning of life. I am so sorry you have had to experience so much in such a little time here. You will forever be my hero. You saved me.

Special thanks to my daughter, Berlyn. Daddy loves you and owes you the world. I will do my best to deliver.

Special thanks to my son, Brandon Jr. (BJ). Daddy loves you. I am so proud that you are growing to be an amazing young man. When God put you in my life it was for a purpose. You brought structure and drive to my mindset. I know you are here to prepare me for my destiny. Since day one till now and forever, I got you!

Special thanks to my son, Bishop. You are a blessing from Oludamare. Just the energy I needed to take on the world.

And many more thanks to my family, Mom, Dad, Sisters, Brothers, friends, followers, and clients who believe in me. I look forward to spreading this message of mental health and perseverance around the world.

For booking, Brandon Ward can be reached at

702.482.2574 www.Iambrandonward.us www.dreamsafe.org

Facebook, Instagram, Twitter

Certified Business Coach, Life Coach, and Motivational Speaker.

Also, pick up "From Tragedy to Testimony."

A family's fight to cope. By Tiffany Ward

&

Brazyl's Safe Ventures

By Tiffany Ward

A NOTE ABOUT THE AUTHOR

Brandon and Tiffany Ward reside in Las Vegas (NV) with there now 4 children. Brandon Jr. Brazyl, Berlyn, and new to the family Baby Bishop. After a brief separation, they have come back together and keep rocking. They continue to uplift the community and have started a Non- Profit 501c3 called **DreamSAFE Project.** DreamSAFE Project assist families whose children are victims of a tragedy. They assist the parents; so that the parents can assist the child.